Breaking New Ground
in U.S. Trade Policy

Breaking New Ground in U.S. Trade Policy

A Statement by the
Research and Policy Committee of the
Committee for Economic Development

Westview Press
BOULDER • SAN FRANCISCO • OXFORD

Copyright © 1991 by Westview Press, Inc.

Published in 1991 in the United States of America by Westview Press, Inc., 5500 Central Avenue, Boulder, Colorado 80301, and in the United Kingdom by Westview Press, 36 Lonsdale Road, Summertown, Oxford OX2 7EW

Library of Congress Cataloging-in-Publication Data
Committee for Economic Development. Research and Policy Committee.
   Breaking new ground in U.S. trade policy : a statement / by the
Research and Policy Committee of the Committee for Economic
Development.
     p. cm.
   ISBN 0-8133-8038-3
   1. United States—Commercial policy. I. Title. II. Title:
Breaking new ground in U.S. trade policy.
HF1455.C63   1991
382′.3′0973–dc20   90-28154
                                                                             CIP

Printed and bound in the United States of America

The paper used in this publication meets the requirements
of the American National Standard for Permanence of Paper
for Printed Library Materials Z39.48-1984.

10   9   8   7   6   5   4   3   2   1

Contents

Responsibility for CED Statements on National Policy

The Committee for Economic Development is an independent research and educational organization of over two hundred business executives and educators. CED is nonprofit, nonpartisan, and nonpolitical. Its purpose is to propose policies that bring about steady economic growth at high employment and reasonably stable prices, increased productivity and living standards, greater and more equal opportunity for every citizen, and improved quality of life for all.

All CED policy recommendations must have the approval of trustees on the Research and Policy Committee. This committee is directed under the bylaws which emphasize that "all research is to be thoroughly objective in character, and the approach in each instance is to be from the standpoint of the general welfare and not from that of any special political or economic group." The committee is aided by a Research Advisory Board of leading social scientists and by a small permanent professional staff.

The Research and Policy Committee does not attempt to pass judgment on any pending specific legislative proposals; its purpose is to urge careful consideration of the objectives set forth in this statement and of the best means of accomplishing those objectives.

Each statement is preceded by extensive discussions, meetings, and exchange of memoranda. The research is undertaken by a subcommittee, assisted by advisors chosen for their competence in the field under study.

The full Research and Policy Committee participates in the drafting of recommendations. Likewise, the trustees on the drafting subcommittee vote to approve or disapprove a policy statement, and they share with the Research and Policy Committee the privilege of submitting individual comments for publication.

Except for the members of the Research and Policy Committee and the responsible subcommittee, the recommendations presented herein are not necessarily endorsed by other trustees or by the advisors, contributors, staff members, or others associated with CED.

RESEARCH AND POLICY COMMITTEE August 1990

Purpose of This Statement

When we began this project nearly a year ago, there was already a pressing need to reexamine U.S. trade policy. A decade of massive trade deficits had raised serious questions about U.S. competitiveness even as the United States faced an array of international economic problems. The challenges on the horizon included the scheduled conclusion of the Uruguay Round of GATT negotiations, the entry into force of the U.S.-Canada Free Trade Agreement, and the European Community's 1992 initiative.

During the course of our study, the world has undergone remarkable changes. Eastern Europe and the Soviet Union began to reject autocracy and have indicated their desire to participate in the world economic system. These developments pose additional questions for the United States, which can and should lead an international response to these breakthroughs with a coherent trade policy.

This complex array of challenges and events has prompted the Committee for Economic Development (CED) to construct a modernized framework for the conduct of U.S. trade policy and to reaffirm its support of the multilateral system of trade. The results of this careful rethinking are set forth in the pages of this book.

A History of Consensus and Leadership

For nearly fifty years, CED has endeavored to build a national consensus on policies that promote vigorous U.S. participation in the expanding international economy.

Early CED statements supporting the Marshall Plan and the Bretton Woods Agreement were followed by statements such as *A New Trade Policy for the United States,* which helped bring about the benchmark Trade Expansion Act of 1962, and *The United States and the European Community: Policies for a Changing World Economy,* which examined U.S. policy toward the initial expansion of the European Community. Most recently, *Finance and Third World Economic Growth* (Westview, 1988) explored issues critical to the development of prosperous economies in the Third World.

In the past decade, as the bilateral trade imbalance with Japan has grown dangerously large, CED has joined with its counterpart, Keizai Doyukai (the Japanese Association of Corporate Executives), to produce a series of reports designed to cultivate better economic relations between the two countries. The most recent of these, *Strengthening U.S.-Japan Economic Relations: An Action Program for the Public and Private Sectors* (1989), outlines specific steps that the business communities and governments of the two countries can take to reduce the bilateral imbalance.

Related CED studies have tackled other issues critical to ensuring U.S. competitiveness as well as promoting international development. *Battling America's Budget Deficits* (1989), *Investing in America's Future* (1988), and *Children in Need: Investment Strategies for the Educationally Disadvantaged* (1987) have all called for policy changes that would, among their other benefits, help to enhance U.S. competitiveness in the changing global marketplace. This issue is still a priority for CED: We feel that the recommendations in this statement are essential to bolstering U.S. competitiveness in the decade, and the century, ahead.

Acknowledgments

I would like to express the deep appreciation of the Research and Policy Committee to Edmund B. Fitzgerald, Chairman of Northern Telecom, Ltd., and Chairman of the Subcommittee on Trade Policy, for his tireless effort and sustained leadership in achieving the focus and consensus that make this report so comprehensive. Credit is also due to Subcommittee Vice-Chairman Joseph Neubauer, Chairman of ARA Services, Inc., and the other members of the Subcommittee (listed on pages ix and x). Their breadth of knowledge about both business and international affairs helped give this report a balanced perspective.

I would like to thank the project director, Dr. Isaiah Frank, William L. Clayton Professor of International Economics at the Johns Hopkins School of Advanced International Studies and director of international economic studies for CED, whose special contribution is noted below. In addition, special thanks go to Project Associate Janet Dewar of Johns Hopkins.

Finally, I would like to thank The Pew Charitable Trusts, Inc., whose generous support made this statement possible.

Dean P. Phypers, Chairman
Research and Policy Committee

Special Acknowledgment

I would like to extend the Committee for Economic Development's special thanks to Dr. Isaiah Frank for his work as project director for the subcommittee that developed *Breaking New Ground in U.S. Trade Policy.*

Isaiah Frank has served as CED's Advisor on International Economic Policy for many years. With the publication of this policy statement, we thought it especially fitting to acknowledge the significant contribution Isaiah has made not only in this statement but over the years to our thinking on international economic issues.

As Chairman of the subcommittee that prepared this report and on behalf of my fellow committee members, I wish to thank Isaiah for the insight, wisdom, and clarity he has brought to CED's endeavors.

Edmund B. Fitzgerald, Chairman
CED Subcommittee on Trade Policy

1

Introduction

As the 1990s dawn, the United States finds itself coping with the economic, political, and even psychological legacy of a decade of international deficits of unprecedented size. It is confronted by more formidable foreign competition across the entire spectrum of tradable goods and services, including those on the leading edge of technology, where U.S. preeminence was virtually unchallenged for decades and mistakenly thought by some to be unchallengeable. The United States faces troubling questions about our will, both as private competitors and as a nation, to make the hard choices necessary to meet this tougher competition successfully, erase the deficits, and rebuild a solid foundation for rising living standards for ourselves and for our children.

In 1988, near the peak of the political turbulence these developments produced, Congress overhauled U.S. trade law. The new law, the Omnibus Trade and Competitiveness Act of 1988, accelerated the momentum of the more aggressive trade policy upon which the Reagan administration embarked in its second term. More than ever before, U.S. trade policy is now focused on remedying conditions of unfair trade that afflict American producers at home and abroad. The new law provides a framework for the development of policy toward unfair trade practices that will continue to evolve for some time to come.

While still digesting the results of the Tokyo Round of multilateral trade negotiations of the 1970s, the United States began to prod its trading partners in the mid-1980s to launch a new round. Frustrated by the lethargic response of the world trading community to the U.S. challenge, the Reagan administration served notice that it would not permit the inertia of the multilateral system to thwart its goals. The United States, it said, was ready to deal with like-minded countries. First Israel and then America's largest trading partner, Canada, stepped forward to conclude bilateral free trade agreements with the United States. These agreements are the first major departures by the United States from a multilateral approach to trade liberalization in more than forty years. The implications of these agreements and the basic question of whether a multilateral approach or some alternative will best serve U.S. interests in the future continue to be assessed.

A new round of multilateral negotiations, christened the Uruguay Round, was eventually launched in 1986. One of its prime missions, in the view of the United States, is to bring within the discipline of international rules several new areas of commerce. One of the most challenging is international investment, which is today inextricably linked to international trade. Even if the Uruguay Round succeeds in bringing new discipline to what negotiators call "trade-related investment measures," the time has come for the world to adopt a comprehensive, integrated approach to international investment issues: a General Agreement on Tariffs and Trade (GATT) for investment. Negotiating such an accord should be a top priority of U.S. international economic policy following the Uruguay Round.

These three key issues—unfair trade, the choice between multilateral and alternative approaches to trade liberalization, and the challenge of negotiating an international investment accord—are the focus of this policy statement. What new policies and approaches should the United States pursue?

In considering appropriate policies, our studies and experience have convinced us that open markets are the best means to achieve broad-based improvements in economic welfare.* Regardless of whether U.S. international accounts are in surplus or deficit, an open world trading system is in this country's interest.

Trade improves welfare by encouraging specialization, a dynamic process in which participants produce the goods and services that they can produce best and buy what others produce best. Market-driven trade improves welfare by encouraging competition, a process that spurs innovation, efficiency, and excellence. Trade also improves welfare over time by forcing countries to face up to the need for adjustment to the inexorable process of change as the world economy evolves.

These three basic ideas—specialization, competition, and adjustment—lead to the key principles that should guide the nation's trade policy. First, trade policy should facilitate the optimal allocation of resources through specialization. Second, trade policy should promote market-based competition rather than impede it. Third, trade policy should facilitate adjustment to change rather than retard it.

Three corollaries follow. First, although circumstances (including the need to protect the national security) will arise that will force the

---

*See memorandum by Franklin A. Lindsay (p. 135).

United States to deviate from the foregoing principles, deviations should not divert us from our long-term commitment to open markets at home and abroad. We must strive to minimize the number and duration of deviations. Second, "strategic intervention" by government to gain international competitive advantage runs counter to the market principles on which the U.S. economy is based and which this country has long espoused internationally. Moreover, it is ill suited to our economy and political system. The belief of proponents of managed trade that the United States can no longer "afford" free trade is misguided, and their prescription that the United States should adopt more interventionist policies would constitute a cure worse than the disease.*

Third, there should be a set of guiding principles for dealing with countries whose trade practices diverge from international norms and adversely affect U.S. interests. To the maximum extent possible, the foreign practices should be dealt with through the GATT remedial process. If the practices are not covered by GATT, the United States should aim to negotiate an appropriate expansion of the GATT rules. If compliance with applicable GATT rules or an expansion of the rules to cover the practices in question is not agreed to by the foreign nation involved, the United States should try to moderate or remove the damaging foreign practices by measures that are themselves market-opening in their impact. If restrictive measures must be employed, they should consist of devices that are market-oriented.

Trade policy is important to U.S. economic growth and broadly rising standards of living. Although trade policy can contribute only marginally to restoring balance in America's external accounts, opening markets at home and abroad can do much to facilitate U.S. economic adjustment, improve our productivity, and enhance our competitiveness.

The U.S. external deficits are primarily a macroeconomic problem rather than a trade problem. They represent an excess of U.S. expenditure over output. The federal budget deficit, combined with traditional levels of private consumption and investment, has meant that as a country, the United States has been living beyond its means. This excess spending spills over into a huge net inflow of foreign products, financed by borrowing savings from countries, such as Japan and Germany, that have current-account surpluses.

An inexcusable fault of our political leaders in the 1980s, both in the executive branch and in Congress, has been their excessive preoccupation with symptoms (i.e., with trade deficits) and their failure to come to grips with the principal underlying cause (i.e., the inadequacy

---

*See memorandum by Harold A. Poling (p. 135).

of U.S. domestic savings, the main element of which is our federal budget deficit). We must do better in the 1990s.

To the extent that trade constitutes any part of the problem, it must be forthrightly addressed by appropriate policies. We should always bring all the policy tools available to us to the task of solving our problems. Equally important, the timely and effective resolution of trade issues is essential to sustain political support for open trade policies that are in the country's interest. But it is important to hold realistic expectations about what trade policy can and cannot achieve.

Unfair Trade Practices

Concern with unfair trade has deep roots in the history of U.S. commercial policy, dating at least from Alexander Hamilton's *Report on Manufactures* in 1791. Campaigning against unfair trade was a central theme of Reagan administration trade policy. But the term *unfair trade* is not used in major international trade agreements, and although it appears in the 1988 trade act, it is not defined. Our understanding of unfair trade and our policies toward it continue to evolve. We focus here on four specific types of unfair trade practices that we think cause most of the troubles.

Dumping and Subsidies

Why should the United States worry about foreign dumping and export subsidies since it benefits from access to lower-cost products? The case for firm action against dumping and subsidies rests on the principle that trade flows should be determined by market forces and on the political reality that unless U.S. trade policy is based on a rule of law that is perceived as fair, it will not muster the political support essential to its survival.

Clearly, then, U.S. producers should have the opportunity to obtain relief from these unfair trade practices. It must be remembered, however, that relief does not come free even if it entails no budgetary expenditures. The cost is borne in the form of higher prices paid by domestic users of the product. Protection for one industry can diminish the competitiveness of another. The United Sates must therefore guard against a proliferation of unfair trade actions that have no basis in rational economic principles but instead are proxies for outright protection.

Dumping. The proliferation of antidumping cases in recent years and the growing reliance on an arbitrary standard—the so-called *constructed-value* standard—for calculating margins of dumping suggest that the antidumping law as now applied has become a back door to protection. To remedy this problem, dumping margins should, whenever possible, be calculated by using actual price comparisons. When price comparisons are not possible and a constructed-value approach must be employed, average *variable* costs should replace average total costs as the basis for determining whether dumping exists.*

Export Subsidies. U.S. exporters are at a disadvantage relative to their competitors in Western Europe and Japan because of concessionary export credits. The U.S. Export-Import Bank's "war chest" of approximately $100 million a year is woefully inadequate to match the mixed credit resources available to exporters from other countries. The best solution would be for major trading nations to ban all export credit subsidies so that no country stands to gain an unfair advantage.

In the meantime, the United States needs to match foreign export credits to persuade its trading partners to negotiate an end to all export credit subsidies. One way to make it easier for Congress to finance an adequately expanded war chest for matching such credits would be to alter the budgetary treatment of the Export-Import Bank. Since defaults on the bank's loans are rare, the budgetary cost of its lending should reflect only the losses represented by interest subsidies, not total lending, as is now the case.

No adequate policy tool exists to address a related problem: the loss of U.S. export sales to competitors whose governments provide export subsidies to promote their sales in *third-country markets.* To combat this unfair practice, the United States should provide a *countervailing subsidy* to match other countries' subsidies. To avoid any budgetary impact and also to discourage America's trading partners from subsidizing exports, the countervailing subsidy should be financed by imposing a special duty on U.S. imports from the subsidizing country. Prior authorization for this duty should be obtained from the Subsidies Committee of GATT in order to avoid triggering a retaliatory spiral.

Agricultural products are exempt from the international ban on export subsidies in large measure because governments have long intervened in agriculture to buffer farmers from wide fluctuations in prices and incomes. Costly domestic support programs create a need to subsidize agricultural exports in order to dispose of the surpluses that supports generate. Therefore, to deal with the root causes of the export-subsidy problem in agriculture, the issue of domestic support programs must be addressed. In the meantime, pressure to reduce domestic government supports should be exerted by including agricul-

---

*See memorandum by Harold A. Poling (p. 135).

tural export subsidies in the ban on export subsidies. A five-year transition period for phasing out agricultural export subsidies should be adopted. Addressing this issue as well as the related problem of agricultural protection is critical to the success of the Uruguay Round.

Domestic Subsidies. Domestic subsidies are a vast gray area. International agreement (GATT) proscribes export subsidies on nonprimary products but permits subsidies that are not specifically related to exports. The only obligation is to try to avoid adverse effects on a country's trading partners. The GATT Subsidies Code goes further, explicitly recognizing the legitimacy of domestic subsidies as instruments of industrial policy.

International discipline over domestic subsidies should be strengthened. First, the Subsidies Code should explicitly identify potentially troublesome domestic subsidies as well as those unlikely to have significant trade-distorting effects. Second, new rules should be developed to provide more effective remedies for the trade-distorting effects of government targeting of particular industries for special assistance and support.

The steel industry provides an excellent example of the multiple economic distortions that can result from a prolonged pattern of subsidization and protection. Because of the importance of steel, countries are unwilling to allow the industry to be fully exposed to international competition; hence, it is one of the most heavily subsidized and protected industries worldwide. Confronted with this situation, the U.S. steel industry has sought relief from foreign unfair trade practices.

Under President Reagan, the United States negotiated a number of *voluntary restraint agreements* (VRAs) to limit foreign exports of certain products to the United States. VRAs are a particularly undesirable form of import protection.* They rigidify patterns of trade by fixing the market share of foreign suppliers, they can produce extraordinary profits (the difference between the protected U.S. price and the world market price) for foreign exporters, and they also can undermine U.S. efforts to strengthen international trade rules and get rid of other countries' restrictions on competitive U.S. products.

CED therefore strongly supports the U.S. government's decision to seek an international consensus on steel trade that would provide effective discipline over government aid and intervention and that would lower barriers to global trade in steel. We also concur with the decision to enforce vigorously the laws against injurious dumping and subsidi-

---

*See memorandum by Harold A. Poling (p. 135).

zation after the VRAs are lifted in 1992. The normal remedy is offsetting tariffs, a less pernicious form of protection than rigid quotas.

Unfair Restrictions on Access to Foreign Markets

The emphasis of U.S. trade policy shifted during the 1980s from combating *unfair imports* through antidumping and countervailing duties to pursuing more open foreign markets for American exporters. The statutory basis for the drive against *unfair foreign market access restrictions* is Section 301 of the Trade Act of 1974.

Section 301 is based on the reasonable principle that the United States should use access to its vast domestic market as leverage to open markets abroad. Indeed, the principle of reciprocity underlies eight rounds of multilateral negotiations to liberalize trade in which the United States has been a leader. However, the way in which the principle is applied in Section 301 departs sharply from tradition. Its main deficiency is its unilateral character. Section 301 can be used to attack foreign practices not illegal under international rules but unilaterally deemed unfair by the United States.*

The threat of retaliation through denial of access to the U.S. market can occasionally serve as an effective strategy to open foreign markets. Used sparingly, bilateral pressure is not necessarily inconsistent with advancing the objectives of a multilateral trading system. At the same time, we must not lose sight of the dangers inherent in aggressive use of Section 301. When the threat of retaliation fails to gain improved access to a foreign market and the United States retaliates by restricting access to the U.S. market, Section 301 has failed. Retaliation provides no remedy for the U.S. exporter, and restricting access of foreign goods to the U.S. market harms the U.S. economy as well as the foreign exporter. Moreover, retaliation can escalate into a destructive cycle of counterretaliation, unraveling past gains in opening markets to the detriment of all trading nations.

For fifty years, the United States has led the world in building a system of international law governing trade in which countries act according to rules. We have not succeeded as well as we would have liked, but great progress has been made. The process of building that system continues today. If the United States now abandons the effort by relying on unilateral judgments of others' actions, it will set a quite different example for the world to emulate. If all countries demand that their trading partners change their laws and practices which are *not*

---

*See memorandum by Harold A. Poling (p. 135).

inconsistent with international rules and retaliate when they refuse, chaos will result.

The United States should be firm in the defense of its interests. It should also be cautious and deliberate, acting not out of frustration and anger in ways that will thwart its long-term objectives but rather in ways calculated to achieve them.

How can unfair restrictions on access to foreign markets be addressed in a way that maximizes the chances for effective redress and that minimizes the need to resort to unilateral retaliation? The answer lies in channeling as many cases as possible to the improved multilateral GATT dispute-settlement facility, on which a consensus has now been reached in the Uruguay Round.

If the United States wants an effective GATT dispute-settlement mechanism—and CED strongly believes that it is in the U.S. interest—we will have to show more good faith by accepting the results of the process when the verdict goes against us. Leadership requires action by example as well as by exhortation.

Intellectual Property Rights

Inadequate protection of intellectual property is an unfair trade practice that displaces sales of legitimate goods and ultimately discourages innovation and investment. Improving protection for intellectual property rights around the world must remain among the highest priorities of U.S. trade policy.

CED therefore welcomes the lead taken by the United States in the Uruguay Round to develop a comprehensive GATT agreement on improved and modernized standards for the protection of intellectual property rights as well as effective procedures for enforcement and dispute settlement. Previous GATT negotiations were focused only on a trademark anticounterfeiting code enforceable at national borders. Some developing countries want to limit the present negotiations in similar fashion, but we believe that would be a mistake. A comprehensive agreement is needed not only to cover the interception of goods bearing counterfeit trademarks at national borders but also to deal promptly with piracy, counterfeiting, and infringement at the source.

CED strongly favors an agreement that covers all intellectual property and provides for enforcement at and beyond national borders. We recommend that the United States and other countries committed to negotiating a comprehensive agreement refuse to water down its provisions in order to attract the support of a greater number of countries who oppose a comprehensive accord.

Competitive Disadvantage Contained in U.S. Law and Regulation

Unfair trade practices normally refer to actions by foreign companies or governments. But a number of serious impediments to the ability of U.S. firms to compete internationally stem from *domestic* laws and regulations. American business views these self-inflicted disadvantages as a kind of unfair trade practice. To improve U.S. competitiveness, we propose reforms in strategic export controls, antitrust law, remedies for corrupt practices, product liability, and U.S. tax law.

Our proposals in the area of strategic export controls are based on the concept of tighter restrictions on a narrower range of truly critical technologies. We endorse efforts to reduce the ambiguities and jurisdictional conflicts in antitrust law and to bring enforcement into conformity with the new realities of the global economy. These efforts are necessary to lower barriers to entry into new markets and to reduce the risks and costs of technology development and joint ventures. We support vigorous pursuit of a comprehensive international agreement on corrupt practices in foreign transactions; this is not a problem that U.S. domestic law alone can address. We endorse changes in the treatment of product liability in international transactions consistent with the principle of national treatment. We urge an early review of the 1986 revisions in the tax treatment of foreign operations of U.S. firms that takes U.S. competitiveness into account.

Multilateral Versus Alternative Approaches

For three and a half decades, the United States pursued a trade policy firmly grounded in the principles of multilateralism. Exceptions were rare. In recent years, however, exceptions have grown in number and importance. The most significant has been the comprehensive free trade agreement negotiated with Canada, America's largest single trading partner.

The tendency toward exceptions has been motivated by a spreading conviction that the single-minded pursuit of multilateralism no longer adequately serves U.S. interests. Frustration with the weaknesses of the multilateral system and the promise of the United States-Canada Free Trade Agreement lend support to a shift in U.S. policy toward the negotiation of additional free trade arrangements. Such arrangements hold the promise of opening key foreign markets to U.S. exports, establishing improved procedures for resolving disputes, and imposing discipline on national policy where no discipline now exists. Such agreements also could tailor U.S. policy to the unique circumstances of important bilateral relationships.

However, our overall experience with discriminatory arrangements and the global scope of U.S. interests offer compelling reasons to be highly skeptical that long-term U.S. interests can adequately be served by a policy that emphasizes discriminatory over multilateral arrangements. Regardless of what might be said to the contrary, the unambiguous signal that a shift in U.S. policy would send to this country's trading partners would be that the United States was abandoning the multilateral trading system. The risks of misunderstandings, commercial disputes with stronger political overtones, and increasing mistrust would almost certainly be greater in a trading system dominated by discriminatory arrangements. Moreover, it is likely to prove impossible to solve some problems of high priority to the United States through bilateral or even plurilateral arrangements with other countries.

The United States will continue to have global economic concerns, and it is therefore in the nation's interest to prevent fragmentation of the world economy. Its global economic interests and leadership role will be enhanced by the evolution of a stronger multilateral, nondiscriminatory trading system. Despite the more equal distribution of power that now characterizes the world economy, there is no country able or willing to replace the United States as the leader of such a system.

We conclude that the highest U.S. trade policy priority for the immediate future must be the successful conclusion of the Uruguay Round of multilateral trade negotiations. A successful round will strengthen the multilateral system, advance the process of trade liberalization, and improve international discipline, thus contributing to the solution of many of the problems that have stimulated interest in discriminatory trading arrangements.

The United States should especially avoid sector-specific trade arrangements. It may be conceptually possible for such arrangements, whether negotiated bilaterally or among a number of countries, to be motivated by trade-liberalizing intentions and to have trade-liberalizing consequences. However, our overwhelming experience has been that such managed trade arrangements are motivated by trade-restricting intentions and have trade-limiting consequences.* This tendency has become, regrettably, an increasingly important one in the global economy.

---

*See memorandum by Harold A. Poling (p. 135).

Europe

The 1992 process of economic integration in Europe should bring substantial benefits to the United States to the extent that it is driven by forces of liberalization and openness. By providing a more unified market with harmonized standards and taxes, it should stimulate faster European growth and lead to increased U.S. exports to and investment in the European Community (EC).

U.S. policy should actively encourage liberalization and openness in the 1992 process and strongly oppose measures that would take the process in a protectionist, "Fortress Europe" direction.* The U.S. should have four objectives: (1) to prevent any erosion of the status quo in terms of U.S. access to the EC market, (2) to ensure full national treatment for the European affiliates of U.S. corporations, (3) to work out mutually acceptable arrangements for participation of European and American companies in one another's cooperative research and experimentation projects, and (4) to work with the EC both directly and in the Uruguay Round to ensure that decisions taken in the 1992 process are compatible with and supportive of multilateral agreements emerging from the round.

Japan and the Pacific Rim

A discriminatory trade agreement between the United States and Japan would be destructive of the multilateral system and would be most unlikely to resolve the problems that lie at the root of the persistent trade friction between the two countries. We strongly advise against a U.S.-Japan free trade agreement. Insofar as the Pacific Rim is concerned, U.S. interests lie in *integrating* the countries of the rim into the *global* trading system and making them a force for constructing a stronger, more effective multilateral system. The special characteristics of U.S. ties to the Pacific Rim may well justify the creation of new forums for consultation and cooperation but not the negotiation of discriminatory trading arrangements.

Mexico

Without a doubt, Mexico deserves special consideration in U.S. trade policy. Market forces are inexorably pushing Mexico and the United States toward closer economic integration. The question is how to shape and influence the course of that integration.

---

*See memorandum by Harold A. Poling (p. 135).

The obstacles to the negotiation of a formal free trade agreement between the United States and Mexico in any short time frame are probably insurmountable. Alternative approaches should be taken. The two governments can continue to address issues on an ad hoc basis in a way that would advance the process of economic integration without trying to define an ultimate goal. A more ambitious approach would be to enter into negotiations aimed at achieving a comprehensive free trade agreement over an extended period of time, with a differential pace of liberalization reflecting the two countries' different levels of economic development. However, given the political sensitivity of the relationship, the United States should defer to Mexico to take the initiative for any negotiations of this type.

Trade and Investment

Despite the close links between trade and investment, there is a fundamental asymmetry in the way in which the two are treated internationally. GATT is a multilateral institution for promoting trade liberalization, a common set of trade rules, and an instrument for resolving trade disputes between nations. Nothing comparable exists for international investment.

What does exist is a patchwork of unilateral, bilateral, and partial multilateral approaches, some of which are seriously misguided. For example, the United States is trying unilaterally to influence the investment policies of a number of developing countries by threatening to reduce their access to the U.S. market. This strategy is highly questionable when foreign country investment practices are not in violation of any international commitment but U.S. denial of market access may be. Bilateral investment treaties hold promise as a tool to advance U.S. interests, but the U.S. approach to negotiating them has been too inflexible. Major emphasis should be placed on dispute settlement, the transfer of funds, and expropriation and compensation. Less emphasis, at least initially, should be placed on the right of establishment and performance requirements. The United States should also be willing to consider applying the national and most-favored-nation principles only to future investment. The optimal solution to international investment problems lies neither in unilateral nor in bilateral approaches, however. It lies in a new multilateral agreement.

Companies throughout the world have become increasingly aware that there is no way to compete internationally except through *both* international investment and trade. Much of world trade is internalized within multinational companies in the form of imports and exports between affiliates of the parent firm. And in much of the rapidly growing services sector, international trade is inseparable from international investment because activities such as banking and insurance usually require an established presence in the foreign country. Moreover, business has become increasingly internationalized through the formation of intercorporate alliances that mix the national identities of firms.

Fortunately, there has been a marked trend toward the liberalization of government policies on foreign direct investment in both developed and developing countries in recent years. But nationalistic opposition to foreign investment is far from dead. In the United States, there has recently been strong pressures to resist Japanese and other foreign investment and to impose discriminatory requirements for their establishment and operation. In the European Community, too, efforts have been made, in conjunction with the formulation of new rules for the single European market, to subject foreign enterprises to discriminatory treatment. In developing countries, the traditional policy of confrontation has been largely replaced by a more pragmatic approach, but the legacy of tradition nevertheless creates problems. Political temptations to play on nationalistic emotions are strong everywhere.

For all these reasons, CED recommends that preparatory steps be taken now to negotiate a comprehensive international investment accord in the Organization for Economic Cooperation and Development (OECD) following the conclusion of the Uruguay Round in 1990. The negotiation would be open not only to members of the OECD but also to any like-minded countries willing to participate. Other non-OECD countries, including developing nations and eventually the centrally planned economies, could apply for accession later as their liberalization efforts mature.

Essential elements of the new accord would include the right of establishment (subject to exceptions for reasons of public order and national security); national treatment; expropriation, compensation, and free transfer of funds (not problems among OECD countries but important for developing countries that may choose to sign); discipline on the use of performance requirements not already covered by GATT; dispute settlement; and a commitment to avoid adopting new foreign investment incentives and disincentives and to phase out existing ones over time.

The Issues

Rights of Establishment. A major obstacle to achieving international agreement on rights of establishment is the need to define what constitutes a legitimate policy reason for restricting foreign investment. Some limits on the scope of foreign enterprise will continue, but such restrictions should be applied on a most-favored-nation basis (i.e., equal treatment for foreign firms regardless of their nationality). Because administrative procedures for screening can themselves be a major deterrent to foreign investment, governments should provide greater clarity in the rules and streamlined procedures for clearance and licenses.

National Treatment. National treatment is the principle that foreign investors, once established in a country, should be treated no less favorably than domestic enterprises with respect to national laws, regulations, and administrative practices. CED endorses the staunch U.S. advocacy of the principle of unconditional national treatment. However, the principle is far from an ironclad guarantee of nondiscrimination. Certain types of regulations, such as limitations on the remittance of profits abroad, may nominally apply to domestic as well as foreign firms, but their impact is overwhelmingly discriminatory in practice. Such discriminatory practices should be eliminated.

Performance Requirements. Performance requirements are conditions imposed by host governments on the entry or operation of foreign enterprises. They comprise a wide variety of measures such as local-content requirements, minimum export levels, technology-transfer obligations, and licensing requirements. By pressuring firms toward economic behavior inconsistent with market forces, they directly or indirectly distort trade and investment flows, lead to uneconomic use of resources, and harm the interests of other countries.

Performance requirements should be made subject to clear international discipline so that those demonstrably damaging to other countries' interests are avoided or removed. Pending the adoption of explicit international rules on performance requirements, the United States should vigorously counter them bilaterally under existing GATT rules when they adversely affect U.S. interests.

Incentives and Disincentives. Investment incentives and disincentives are the principal mechanism for enforcing such requirements. The only multilateral undertaking on this subject, within the OECD, has had little deterrent effect on the use of special inducements to attract foreign direct investment. An effort to craft a more effective deterrent should be part of any general attempt to negotiate a multilateral convention on foreign direct investment.

Transfer of Remittances. Early liberalization and ultimate elimination of the restrictions on remittances would serve the interests of both companies and the developing countries. It would reduce a major obstacle to new flows of foreign investment at a time when private commercial lending has virtually ceased for many debt-ridden developing countries desperately in need of additional capital to restore acceptable rates of economic growth.

Expropriation and Compensation. Given the improved climate for foreign investment and the reduced risk of nationalization, the prospects are favorable for the inclusion of certain basic principles on expropriation in any new international investment code. The principles should acknowledge the sovereign right of governments to expropriate private property for a public purpose. But they should specify that in the event of expropriation of a foreign enterprise, the action should be subject not only to due process under the laws of the host country but also to the internationally accepted standard of prompt, adequate, and effective compensation.

U.S. Foreign Investment Concerns

Inward Investment. Between 1980 and 1988, the stock of foreign direct investment in the United States multiplied fourfold compared with an increase of only 50 percent in the stock of U.S. direct investment abroad. Europe accounts for 66 percent and Japan for 16 percent, but the rate of growth of investment originating in Japan has outstripped the flows from Europe over the past eight years.

The steep increase in inflows of foreign direct investment in recent years has given rise to fears that foreigners are "buying up" America. Concerns expressed about U.S. loss of control of its own economic destiny echo the cries heard over the years in Canada and many developing countries about the impact of U.S. investment there. This subject needs to be placed in perspective.

At the end of 1988, U.S. companies' investments in their foreign affiliates ($327 billion) were almost equal to foreign direct investment in this country ($329 billion). However, because the statistics are based on book rather than market value, they greatly understate the comparative value of U.S. investment, which is on average of older vintage than foreign investment in the United States. This understatement is reflected in the fact that earnings on U.S. direct investment abroad in 1988 were more than four times the earnings on foreign direct investment in this country.

From the standpoint of limiting volatility in financial markets, it is surely better to have a share of the U.S. current-account deficit financed by direct investment, implying a long-term commitment to the U.S. economy, than entirely through the acquisition by foreigners of liquid financial assets. A sudden large liquidation of foreign assets could have highly adverse effects on the U.S. economy by sharply weakening the dollar and exerting strong upward pressure on interest rates.

Apart from contributing to financial stability, foreign direct investment in the United States brings the benefits that this country, as the world's largest investor abroad, has long cited as advantages for the host country: the increased output generated by the transfer of additional resources to the United States (in the form of capital, technology, and management) and their productive use. The rewards of this increased output accrue to domestic labor in the form of higher wages and to the country as a whole in the form of improved technology and skills, sharpened competition, new export opportunities, and larger tax revenues for the government.

Outward Investment. Concerns about foreign direct investment are not confined to inward flows. Feàrs have also been expressed that U.S. investment abroad leads to the loss of production, exports, and jobs for the U.S. economy.

The belief that in the absence of U.S. investment abroad, production at home would be preserved or increased is unrealistic. Much U.S. investment abroad serves host-country markets when exporting from the United States is not feasible because of the need to integrate production, marketing, and after-sales service in the local market or because of foreign import barriers or other factors. U.S. investment abroad can also become necessary to serve U.S. or third-country markets when fundamental shifts in relative costs render production in the United States uncompetitive. In both situations, U.S. production is not a viable alternative. Moreover, if American firms do not make such investments, foreign firms will. It is also important to note that the foreign affiliates of U.S. firms are substantial purchasers of capital goods and components produced in the United States.

Apart from security safeguards now in effect, restrictions on inward or outward foreign investment can play no useful role in the increasingly integrated global economy in which the United States must compete. Proposals to adopt such restrictions should be strongly resisted by U.S. policy makers.

Conclusion

As the 1990s begin, the nation stands at a critical juncture in its trade policy. In the face of stubborn external deficits, worries about U.S. competitiveness, and concerns over foreign unfair trade practices, we hear persistent demands for government "management" of trade, "strategic" government intervention to nurture selected industries, the abandonment of multilateralism and the embrace of discriminatory trade deals, and an end to this country's long-standing policy of openness to foreign investment. We hear these demands, and we unequivocally reject them.

We have chosen to focus on three areas—unfair trade, multilateralism, and foreign investment—that we believe lie at the heart of many of today's trade policy controversies. There certainly are other important issues, including, for example, the problems of trade in services and agriculture (to which we make considerable reference in this statement but which we do not address in a comprehensive way) and the trade policy consequences of the stunning process of economic opening and reform in the Soviet Union and Eastern Europe (to which we make only passing reference). They, too, deserve careful analysis.

In the pages that follow, we devote considerable attention to the principles that should guide U.S. trade policy. These may seem self-evident to many readers, but the proliferation of legislative gimmickry and demands for ad hoc policy making persuade us that a return to fundamentals is not inconsistent with breaking new ground. For many readers, this will be new ground.

Finally, we couch a number of our recommendations in terms of preferable outcomes in the Uruguay Round of multilateral trade negotiations, which is scheduled to conclude at the end of 1990. Regardless of the results of the Uruguay Round, however, these recommendations are appropriate objectives of U.S. trade policy. If they are not realized in the round, the United States should continue to pursue them. CED is convinced that if its recommendations are implemented, they will make a major contribution to improving the global regime governing trade and advance the interests of the United States in the decade ahead.*

---

*See memorandum by James D. Houghton and John D. Ong (p. 136).

2

The Evolving
Global Landscape

As the 1990s begin, pathbreaking developments are unfolding that underline the need for the United States to rethink basic elements of its trade policy: the scheduled conclusion of the Uruguay Round of the General Agreement on Tariffs and Trade negotiations in 1990, the European Community's program to achieve a single internal market by 1992, and the entry into force of the new U.S.-Canada Free Trade Agreement.

Transcending these discrete events are fundamental longer-term trends that will condition the environment for world trade in the 1990s and beyond. One trend is the accelerating globalization of markets not only for goods but for services, capital, and technology as well. This development and some of its implications for public policy are the subjects of CED's recent publication, *New Dynamics in the Global Economy.*[1]

A second trend is the extraordinary worldwide shift in both ideology and policy in favor of market-driven rather than government-directed solutions to national economic problems, a change that is taking hold in much of the developing world and in most of the centrally planned economies of Eastern Europe and Asia. To the extent that national economies are increasingly shaped by market forces, they inevitably become fuller participants in world trade and in the international economic system more generally.

The most stunning developments that give evidence of this trend are occurring in Eastern Europe. To say that a revolution is under way is no exaggeration. The shape of Europe is changing rapidly. The stark economic and political divisions between East and West that have stood immutable for more than forty years are eroding. The crumbling of the Berlin Wall is a metaphor for what is coming in the realms of economics and politics.

How far and how fast the changes will come is impossible to predict, but it is already clear that they will have major implications for the world economy and for U.S. trade policy. The issue of extending most-favored-nation tariff treatment is already widely under discussion. The participation of the Soviet Union and the countries of Eastern Europe in the GATT and in future rounds of multilateral trade negotiations will need to be addressed. And the implications of these developments for "1992" and the ultimate meaning of European economic integration are now open questions.

The task of grappling with all these issues is one policy makers should take up with enthusiasm because of the promise inherent in them. That promise is the evolution of a more interdependent world economy increasingly reliant upon market forces and increasingly free of discrimination and the control of governments.

Finally, the North-South divide has become more and more blurred as many developing countries have proven capable of rapidly absorbing modern technology. Increasingly, they have been diversifying their economies away from heavy concentration on primary commodities and are becoming significant producers and exporters of manufactured products as well.

Trade Policy and U.S. Competitiveness

From a strictly U.S. perspective, concern about trade has been intensified by the rapidly rising U.S. current-account deficit[2] during the 1980s. Although the deficit dropped back somewhat from its 1987 peak of $154 billion (3.4 percent of the gross national product [GNP]) to $127 billion (2.6 percent of GNP) in 1988, its future trend is clouded. Just as the budget deficit is generally viewed as our primary domestic economic problem, so the current-account deficit is our principal international economic problem.[3] Moreover, the stubborn persistence of the external deficit (despite the sharp reversal since 1985 of much of the large appreciation of the dollar that occurred in the first half of the 1980s) is often cited as symptomatic of much that is fundamentally wrong with the U.S. economy. The condition is commonly summed up as a loss of U.S. competitiveness.

Competitiveness is a slippery term. Its meaning is clearer for a firm than for a nation. If a firm is not competitive, it is likely to go out of business. But countries do not go out of business. What, then, do we mean by the competitiveness of a country such as the United States?

Competitiveness is the ability of a country to achieve a sustainable trade balance in goods and services combined while providing an acceptable rate of improvement in the living standard of its people. Both criteria are essential. During the 1980s, the American standard of living has been rising, but at the cost of unsustainable trade deficits that have converted the nation from the world's largest creditor to the world's largest debtor in absolute terms (though not in relation to GNP).[4] On the other hand, a country's trade may move into balance or even into surplus, but at the cost of a declining standard of living. For example, from 1980 to 1986, Bolivia experienced large export surpluses, but its per capita income fell sharply. The country was compelled to run trade surpluses in order to service the large external debts it had previously incurred, but the burden of the real transfer of resources to foreign creditors contributed to the decline in the nation's productive capacity.[5]

A program to restore U.S. competitiveness must be based on three elements:

- Macroeconomic policies to eliminate the external deficit by reorienting the U.S. economy away from consumption and government spending toward private investment and exports
- Longer-term policies to raise lagging productivity in order to minimize the effect on U.S. living standards of the need to bring domestic spending back into line with domestic production while providing the real resources needed to service the foreign debt
- Trade and trade-related policies to achieve and maintain open access to foreign markets for U.S. exports and investment while avoiding protectionism at home that would insulate domestic industries from foreign competition and adversely affect U.S. productivity

Of the three sets of policies required to restore U.S. competitiveness, two—macroeconomic and productivity policies—have already been studied in detail by CED. A summary of the remedial actions we have recommended is presented in the recent CED policy statement *Investing in America's Future* (1988).[6]

On the macroeconomic side, the principal measure required is the elimination of the U.S. budget deficit over the next several years through a responsible combination of expenditure restraints and tax increases. Along with expenditure *reduction*, additional expenditure *switching* from foreign to domestic products may be necessary through a further downward adjustment in the exchange value of the dollar. Complementary expansionary measures are needed in the trade surplus countries, not only Japan and Germany but also Taiwan, Korea, and a number of the smaller European countries.[7]

In order to improve the relatively slow growth in U.S. productivity in recent years, public policy measures are necessary to increase the incentives for saving and investment. We must substantially reverse the serious lag in the U.S. saving rate,[8] which is well below that of our principal trading partners. In addition, public and private policy measures must be taken to promote technological progress through research and development and more effective commercial application of new discoveries. U.S. firms operating in trade-sensitive fields will need to push hard to keep improving the appeal and price competitiveness of their products. High priority should also be given to strengthening this country's human capital base through upgrading the education of its young people.

The third element in a program to restore U.S. competitiveness is trade policy in its broadest sense. *Trade policy* refers to government measures that have industry-specific applications. Whether or not applied at the border, they significantly affect international commerce in both goods and services, international investment, and the protection of intellectual property rights. Under a regime of flexible exchange rates, trade policy tends to affect primarily the level and composition of a nation's trade rather than the overall balance between its exports and imports. These compositional effects can be very serious; for certain industries, having access to foreign markets can be the difference between success and failure. In short, to the extent that trade policy results in more open markets at home and abroad, it contributes to a more efficient use of a nation's resources and therefore to higher productivity and an improved standard of living. In this sense, trade policy is linked to the U.S. economy's competitiveness.[9]

The Role of Trade in the World Economy

In considering trade policy, our studies and experience have convinced us that the maintenance of open markets is the best route to achieving broad-based improvements in economic welfare. The logic for this proposition lies in the nature of trade itself. Trade contributes to economic welfare because of two dynamics inherent in the process of international exchange: specialization and competition.

Specialization

How countries benefit from trade can be illustrated by an analogy to individuals. Take a highly skilled engineer who is also a first-rate carpenter and plumber. Even though the engineer may be capable of building a house for himself, it makes little sense for him to do so. Rather it makes sense for him to concentrate on selling his engineering services, an endeavor that optimizes his skills and for which he receives the greatest financial reward, and to purchase carpentry and plumbing services from others. By specializing in what he does best as determined by the market, the engineer maximizes his welfare. Likewise, the carpenter and plumber, by specializing in what they do best, are able to maximize their welfare.

The same basic logic applies to trade between countries. Of course, countries import some goods because it may be the only way to obtain them. However, even if a country were capable of producing everything its citizens needed or wanted, trading would still make sense. The reason is that a country can produce some things better than other things; that is, it has a comparative advantage in producing certain products and services. It makes sense for countries to specialize in producing what they make best and to buy from others the products and services that others make best.[10] Specialization enables the participants in trade to achieve economies of scale and to optimize the use of their resources, thereby maximizing their economic welfare.

Competition

The dynamic of competition also enhances economic welfare. Competition between producers in different countries spurs them to achieve excellence. It motivates innovation and investment. It also motivates producers to minimize costs and to exercise restraint in setting prices.

Adjustment to Change

One of the most important characteristics of the world economy is its dynamism. What products are made and how they are made are constantly changing in response to new technological developments. Nations' economies also evolve over time at different rates and in different ways. As a result, the comparative advantage of countries shifts. Such change is inevitable. Successful adjustment to this dynamic of change is essential if a nation is to ensure a rising standard of living for its people.

These three fundamental concepts—**specialization, competition,** and **adjustment**—lead us to the key strategic principles that should guide trade policy. First, trade policy should facilitate the optimal allocation of a country's resources through efficient specialization. Second, trade policy should promote competition rather than impede it. Third, trade policy should facilitate adjustment to change rather than retard it.

Trade Policy

In a market economy that functioned perfectly, there would be no need for government intervention in trade except possibly for reasons of national security. Prices would guide the optimal allocation of resources. Open competition would prevail. The factors of production, including labor, would be perfectly mobile within countries, and the process of adjustment would be smooth and prompt. But the world economy is not perfect, and trade policy is necessary.

Apart from national security, there are two broad categories of justifications for trade policy: (1) to correct for distortions in the operation of market forces (i.e., neutralizing or obtaining the elimination of foreign trade barriers or other government interventions that distort competition), and (2) to provide temporary import relief to facilitate the adjustment process, which is rarely smooth and often involves dislocation and pain for those affected by it.

The Issue of Protection

Debates in the United States over when and in what circumstances import competition should be restrained almost always boil down to a question of "us" (the United States) versus "them" (foreign producers). That is understandable, but the real issue is better defined as "us" versus "us." Restricting import competition has adverse consequences for the U.S. economy that often are equal to or greater than the price that foreigners pay for those restrictions. In fact, as recent experience (restrictions on automobile trade being a classic example) has shown, foreign producers sometimes gain huge windfalls from U.S. import restrictions.

Whenever a country restricts market-driven trade to substitute domestic production for imports, two consequences inevitably follow: The first is a loss to the economy that occurs because resources will no longer be optimally utilized. This loss of efficiency is a consequence of the retreat from specialization that trade restraints bring. The second is a transfer of income from consumers to the domestic producers of the protected product. If domestic producers were as efficient as foreign producers, there would be no reason to restrict market-driven imports in the first place. Restrictions on trade lead to higher prices that domestic consumers must pay domestic producers for the same product they could otherwise buy from foreign countries at a lower cost.

Therefore, the way to view protection is mainly in terms of who in the United States benefits from protection and who pays its cost, rather than in terms of U.S. interests versus foreign interests.

The Political Economy of Trade Policy

It should be intuitively clear that the beneficiaries of trade protection are narrow, concentrated interests: the producers of the protected goods.

They gain at the expense of consumers when the protected products are goods such as clothing or bicycles sold directly to individuals. When the goods protected are themselves used in the production of other products, such as steel or machine tools, both the industries that consume those goods and the ultimate consumers lose.

Generally speaking, the balance of raw political power in debates over protection favors the advocates of protection. Take textiles and clothing as an example. For producers of textiles and clothing, obtaining protection from imports may make the difference between profit and loss and may even affect the very existence of some firms. That is powerful motivation to organize and pressure the government to intervene to restrict imports. For consumers, however, paying higher prices for sheets and shirts may be distressing (presuming consumers know protection is increasing the prices of the products they buy), but it is unlikely to be important enough to any individual consumer to justify organizing and pressuring the government not to restrict imports.

Thus, the debate over protection is for the most part not fought on a level playing field. The field is tilted to the advantage of the advocates of protection.

The Struggle to Control Trade Policy

The political economy of trade explains the long-standing struggle between the executive branch and Congress for primacy in trade policy. The Constitution grants Congress, not the President, the power to regulate domestic and foreign commerce. But Congress learned a hard lesson in the early 1930s, when it enacted the infamous Smoot-Hawley Tariff that stifled trade and prolonged the Great Depression: that it was ill suited to conduct trade policy. So, beginning in 1934, Congress turned over to the President the task of managing the nation's trade policy. Almost ever since, however, Congress has been struggling to regain control. Every major trade bill Congress has passed over the past three decades has circumscribed the President's authority and discretion to pursue an open trade policy. This struggle lay just beneath the surface of almost all the debates over the most controversial provisions of the Omnibus Trade and Competitiveness Act of 1988.

As a body composed of representatives of limited geographic constituencies, Congress is more vulnerable to the pressures exerted by concentrated special interests in debates over trade protection than the President, whose constituency is national. Debates over the years on the question of whether the United States should restrict imports for the most part have not pitted Democrats against Republicans but, rather, the executive branch against Congress.[11]

Rationale for Multilateral Trade Negotiations

Even though countries would benefit from unilaterally reducing their import barriers, they have rarely done so, primarily because of concentrated political pressure from the industries that gain from protection. The only practical way of accomplishing substantial trade liberalization, therefore, has been in the context of a multilateral negotiation. That setting makes it possible to mobilize domestic *export* industries in support of liberalization because the reduction of a country's import barriers becomes the quid pro quo for opening foreign markets for its exporters. The more numerous the negotiating partners, the greater the opportunities for opening markets through reciprocal reductions of import barriers. Therefore, a multilateral negotiation makes it possible to supplement the weak consumer influence in combatting protection by bringing to bear the pressures of the more dynamic export industries as a counterweight to domestic protectionist forces.

GATT

The General Agreement on Tariffs and Trade is the principal multilateral instrument through which the United States has sought to improve the world trading system. GATT has three functions: to sponsor multilateral negotiations for the reduction of trade barriers, to establish and administer a set of rules for the conduct of international trade, and to provide facilities for the settlement of trade disputes.

Although GATT is a long and complicated document, it is based on comparatively few fundamental principles: nondiscrimination in trade, national treatment on internal taxation and regulation, the use of tariffs rather than quotas for the protection of domestic industry, the avoidance of unfair trade practices such as dumping and subsidization, and a willingness to enter into multilateral negotiations for the reciprocal reduction of trade barriers.

Many exceptions and qualifications to these principles are also included in GATT, but the three most important are: the escape clause permitting temporary protection for particular industries injured by imports, the exception for balance-of-payments reasons to the no-quota rule, and the exception to nondiscrimination for countries entering into comprehensive free trade areas or customs unions.

The current Uruguay Round, the latest in the series of GATT negotiations, is an effort to strengthen GATT and to adapt it to the dramatically changing realities in the world economy. A major U.S. objective in the Uruguay Round is to bring under GATT discipline subjects not explicitly covered, including trade in services, intellectual property rights, and trade-related investment measures. The United

States also seeks to strengthen existing GATT rules on subjects such as agricultural trade and subsidies.

Since its inception in 1948, GATT has sponsored eight rounds of multilateral negotiations for which the United States has been the driving force. As a consequence, steady progress has been made in reducing trade barriers worldwide and introducing greater discipline in the international trading system as a whole. During this period, world trade has increased far more rapidly than world production, resulting in a more integrated global economy that has brought great benefit to all nations.

Tactical Principles for Dealing with Trade Policy Issues

Our studies of both scholarly research and practical experience convince us that the following three tactical principles ought to guide U.S. policy makers as they strive to deal with the important trade issues of the day.

First, regardless of whether U.S. international accounts are in surplus or deficit, an open world trading system is in this country's long-term interest. Although circumstances may arise that force the United States to deviate from its liberal trade principles temporarily, they should not divert it from its long-term commitment to open markets at home and abroad. This policy remains the best vehicle to enable the United States to use resources more efficiently, boost economic growth, and raise living standards.

Second, "strategic intervention" by the government to gain international competitive advantage is not in the U.S. interest. It runs counter to the market principles on which the U.S. economy is based and that this country has long espoused for the international trading system as represented by GATT. Moreover, it is ill suited to this nation's economy and political system. Public policy in the United States reflects more the interplay of domestic interests than independent, technocratic decision making. Whereas proponents of managed trade argue that this country can no longer "afford" free trade and should adopt more interventionist domestic and trade policies, CED believes such policies would fail, impeding rather than enhancing our economic vitality.

Third, we recognize that in some circumstances U.S. policy makers may have to deal with countries that are not themselves following the same guiding principles and that are operating outside the bounds of GATT. These circumstances call for more complex tactical principles. If the foreign practices involved are covered by GATT, they should be dealt with through the improved GATT remedial process. If the practices are not covered by the current GATT rules, our primary recourse should be to negotiate an appropriate expansion of GATT to cover the country or the practice in question. Even when that process fails (i.e., when the appropriate expansion of GATT coverage cannot be achieved, or when the offending country does not comply with the relevant GATT rules or remedies), we urge our policy makers to deviate from the foregoing guiding principles only when U.S. interests are being significantly damaged and only in ways that do not violate our GATT obligations. In such circumstances, we believe the best tactical principle for the United States to follow is to try to moderate or remove the damaging foreign practices by measures that are themselves market-opening in their impact. If restrictive measures must be employed, they should consist of devices that are market-oriented (e.g., temporary tariffs rather than quotas because tariffs work through the price system).

In this statement, we apply these three tactical principles in recommending ways to deal with three key trade policy issues that we believe are particularly timely and warrant special attention:

- The concept of unfair trade, which is the centerpiece of the Omnibus Trade and Competitiveness Act of 1988 and which was vigorously extended during the Reagan years from dumping and subsidization to unfair practices abroad and the lack of reciprocity in U.S. access to foreign markets; (the concept of unfair trade applies not only to merchandise trade but to trade in both financial and nonfinancial services and transfers of intellectual property).
- The question of whether the United States should supplement its traditional multilateral approach to trade policy through GATT by entering into separate agreements with smaller groups of countries or with individual countries, as has already been done with Israel and Canada.
- The need to widen the scope of multilateral trading rules by taking into account the closer linkages between trade in goods and services, international investment, and intellectual property.

Notes

1. William J. Beeman and Isaiah Frank, *New Dynamics in the Global Economy* (New York: Committee for Economic Development, 1988).

2. The current-account deficit is a composite of the trade balance on goods and services plus unilateral transactions. Although the deficit in the overall current account in 1988 was $127 billion, the service component registered a surplus of $23 billion.

3. As we debate the implications of the external deficit and appropriate policy responses, we should be mindful of considerable shortcomings in the

data reporting U.S. trade. For example, some experts believe U.S. service exports are vastly understated because U.S. firms do not report their transactions fully. According to this view, full reporting could lead us to a very different understanding of the magnitude of the U.S. external deficit.

4. Although U.S. net external liabilities are five times those of Brazil, the largest debtor among the developing countries, our liabilities in relation to GNP are only one-fifth those of Brazil.

5. George Hatsopoulos, Paul Krugman, and Lawrence Summers, "U.S. Competitiveness: Beyond the Trade Deficit," *Science,* 241 (July 15, 1988), p. 299.

6. See also CED policy statements *Productivity Policy: Key to the Nation's Economic Future* (1983) and *Toll of the Twin Deficits* (1987).

7. The obligation of surplus countries to contribute to an improved world payments balance is implicit in the International Monetary Fund's Articles of Agreement (Article VII, Section 3, the "scarce currency" clause).

8. U.S. personal savings as a percentage of disposable income declined from 9.3 percent in 1973–1974 to 3.8 percent in 1986–1988. The estimated increase in the first quarter of 1989 to a 5.8 percent annual saving rate still leaves U.S. individuals far behind their counterparts abroad, especially in Japan and West Germany, even after allowance for measurement differences. Council of Economic Advisers, *Economic Indicators* (Washington, D.C.: U.S. Government Printing Office, May 1989).

9. Opening markets abroad is an essential element of trade policy. In today's global market, however, U.S. export performance depends on more than access to foreign markets. For example, it requires the elimination of export disincentives contained in U.S. law and regulation, the matching by the U.S. government of concessionary export credits granted by other governments, and official nonfinancial assistance to small and medium-sized companies in such forms as market intelligence and information about potential foreign partners. Equally important, successful exporting requires much greater effort on the part of U.S. private firms to equip themselves to extend their commercial horizons beyond the traditional domestic market. Selling and investing abroad require, among other things, a knowledge of foreign languages and sensitivity to national cultural differences.

10. A country's ability to do certain things best may in some cases be due to government assistance to a particular industry (i.e., a contrived comparative advantage).

11. At times, however, the political parties have championed conflicting philosophies on trade, and party strategists are always vigilant to identify issues, trade among them, that they might exploit to partisan advantage in election campaigns.

3

Unfair Trade

Worldwide attention was focused on the announcement on May 25, 1989, by Carla Hills, the current U.S. Trade Representative, of plans to implement the so-called Super 301 provisions of the Omnibus Trade and Competitiveness Act of 1988 requiring the identification of trade liberalization priorities. The act requires the listing of foreign countries where trade barriers and distortive trade practices are pervasive and significantly impede U.S. exports.

However, the concern with unfair trade is not new. It has deep roots in the history of U.S. commercial policy. From Alexander Hamilton's *Report on Manufactures* in 1791 through debates in the early 1900s about the need for a "scientific" tariff to equalize costs of production at home and abroad, the notion of unfairness has had powerful appeal as a justification for protectionism.

In recent years, the massive U.S. trade deficit gave rise to a new wave of concern over foreign unfair trade practices and proposals for dealing with them, exemplified by the Gephardt amendment.[1] Although this highly protectionist provision was dropped in the end from the Omnibus Trade and Competitiveness Act of 1988, it had garnered enough support to pass the House of Representatives in 1987.

The Reagan administration opposed the Gephardt amendment, but it launched its own campaign against foreign unfair trade practices, utilizing the tools provided by existing laws and the leverage of access to America's domestic market. In one of his last official statements, President Reagan proclaimed the administration's accomplishments in this field.

We have been using every tool that our existing international commitments allow to pry open foreign markets. We've become the first Administration ever to initiate unfair trade practice cases—not waiting for industry to take the first step. And not long ago, we added up all the cases—Administration and industry initiated—and found that during this

Administration, the United States had challenged more unfair trade practices than in any other administration in its history. And from agricultural ·
products and legal services to construction contracts in Japan, to insurance
and intellectual property in Korea, to agricultural trade with Europe,
we've got results. Markets have been opened.

Four decades ago, America accounted for half of the world economy. We
were so big compared to everyone else that we could ignore most unfair
trade practices abroad. Today we're down to about a quarter. And it's
time for everyone to play by the rules if they want to play with us.[2]

In a fact sheet accompanying that speech, the Reagan administration
acknowledged that unfair trade practices have been responsible for only
a fraction of the U.S. trade deficit. Macroeconomic policies have been
far more important. Indeed, the principal impediment to U.S. exports
during the first half of the 1980s arose out of the mismatch of macroeconomic policies at home and abroad—expansionary fiscal policies
in the United States coinciding with contractionary policies in Japan
and Germany. The result was high U.S. interest rates that led to massive
inflows of foreign capital and the extreme appreciation of the dollar.
Most U.S. producers considered the high dollar the single most unfair
condition they faced during the early 1980s, and it had devastating
effects on the competitive position of a host of American industries
both at home and abroad. But a mismatch of macroeconomic policies
leading to an overvalued currency can hardly be called an unfair trade
practice. What, then, do we mean by that expression?

Nowhere in GATT nor in the international codes negotiated under
its auspices is the term "unfair trade practices" used. Although the
expression does appear in the Omnibus Trade and Competitiveness Act
of 1988, it is not given any precise definition. Rather than to attempt
a comprehensive definition in this statement, we believe it is more
practical to focus on four types of microeconomic measures that are
widely regarded by American businessmen as constituting unfair trade
practices: (1) foreign dumping and subsidizing of exports to the United
States or third-country markets, (2) unreasonable foreign restrictions on
access to markets abroad (the main focus of Section 301), (3) violations
of intellectual property rights, and (4) conditions imposed on American
firms by the U.S. government itself that place them at a competitive
disadvantage to foreign firms.

Dumping and Subsidization

The earliest types of unfair trade practices to be condemned in U.S.
law are dumping and subsidization. A countervailing duty law to combat

export subsidies was originally enacted in 1897, and an antidumping law was passed by Congress in 1916.

Export subsidization and dumping are similar in that both generally entail selling abroad at lower prices than at home. However, both practices can occur without price discrimination between domestic and foreign markets. For example, subsidization can occur through preferential export credits. And under certain circumstances, dumping may be deemed to exist, regardless of price discrimination, when foreign sales take place below the cost of production in the exporting country.

The main difference between subsidization and dumping is that the former involves some measure of government support, whereas the latter need not. Often the two practices are linked. The connection is clearest in the case of state-owned enterprises that are enabled by government subsidies to increase their sales abroad at low prices. But dumping can also be encouraged through more indirect measures of public support, such as import restrictions, which provide a captive, high-price home market as a base from which to compete abroad at lower prices. Much of Japanese dumping, when the yen appreciated after 1985, would appear to fall into this category.[3]

Why should we worry about foreign dumping and export subsidization? One argument is that, however adverse these practices may be to producers of like products in the importing country, the nation as a whole benefits from access to lower-cost products. The standard counterargument is that dumping and subsidization can be predatory: once foreigners wipe out domestic competition and take over the market, they will raise prices to monopoly levels and victimize domestic consumers. However, in today's global economy the availability of alternative suppliers should reduce the likelihood of predatory pricing leading to the monopolization of a market.

Nevertheless, the case for firm counteraction against dumping and subsidization remains strong. It rests less on the traditional predatory-pricing argument than on the simple principle on which GATT is based: that trade flows should be determined mainly by comparative advantage and market forces rather than by government intervention. Moreover, unless the international trading regime is based on a rule of law that is perceived as fair, it will not muster the political support essential to its survival.

Implicitly, the GATT treatment of export subsidies and dumping reflects a compromise between the principle that export subsidies should be outlawed and dumping offset and the practical recognition that consumers benefit from the lower prices. Thus, export subsidies on manufactured products are prohibited, and dumping is condemned. But countries do not automatically have the right to take offsetting measures when sales at "less than fair value" take place. The right to impose countervailing or antidumping duties is contingent on the additional finding of material injury to a domestic industry. In the absence of a demonstration of material injury to producers, consumers are able to benefit from the lower prices.

U.S. law is broadly consistent with the GATT articles on dumping and subsidies and with the international codes negotiated under its auspices. Administration of the statutes is divided between the Department of Commerce, which is responsible for the determination of "less than fair value," and the International Trade Commission (ITC), which is responsible for the finding of material injury to domestic producers of the like product.

Recent U.S. legislation is designed primarily to streamline the administration of countervailing and antidumping measures and to expedite their enforcement by shortening the time limit for the various stages in the complex process of applying the laws. The Omnibus Trade and Competitiveness Act of 1988 added a number of technical amendments designed to tighten U.S. law. For example, in determining whether dumped or subsidized imports have caused material injury to domestic producers of like products, the ITC is to make its finding only in the context of production operations in the United States. The fact that a company's foreign operations may be booming is now specifically declared to be irrelevant. The act also made a number of changes in the antidumping laws as they apply to nonmarket economies.

In providing relief from injury due to import competition, U.S. law draws a number of legitimate distinctions between unfair trade competition (i.e., illegal dumping and subsidization) and fairly priced imports (where the only "crime" is that the foreign producer is too competitive). Three such distinctions are especially significant. The first relates to the injury standard. In the case of unfair competition, the standard of material injury needs to be met. However, Section 201 escape-clause actions dealing with fair competition require a demonstration of "serious injury" from imports of fairly priced products.

The second distinction concerns the factors to be taken into account in determining whether to grant relief. In cases of dumping and export subsidies, the only considerations are whether sales have occurred at less than fair value and whether material injury to a domestic producer has occurred. In escape-clause cases, however, the ITC submits its recommendations to the President, who is then obliged to take into account the broader public interest transcending that of the producers alone. This broader context includes the impact on taxpayers, consumers, and communities; the effect on competition in the U.S. market;

the consequences of paying compensation to trading partners if U.S. international obligations require it; and U.S. national security interests.

The third distinction concerns differences in the permissible forms of import relief. For unfair trade practices, the law mandates offsetting tariffs in the form of antidumping and countervailing duties. In escape-clause cases, however, the President is given a wider range of options, including quotas, orderly marketing agreements, and trade adjustment assistance, as well as tariff increases.

What these distinctions imply is that the quest for import relief is easier under the unfair trade statutes than under the escape clause. The former entail less stringent standards of injury, take into account only the producer interest and avoid broader economic and political considerations of national interest, and are administered largely within the bureaucratic apparatus of the Department of Commerce and the ITC without the involvement of the President.[4] Given a choice, therefore, U.S. producers seeking import relief would naturally prefer the route of unfair trade statutes.

This observation is consistent with the record of the small number of actions taken under the escape clause in recent years compared with the flood of cases under the U.S. unfair trade laws. From 1980 to 1986, only 14 escape-clause cases were initiated, and relief was granted in only 5 cases. During the same period, 350 antidumping actions were initiated, resulting in 195 affirmative findings; and 281 antisubsidy cases were initiated, leading to 181 affirmative determinations.[5] In total, during that seven-year period, some form of relief was granted under the unfair trade statutes in 376 cases, compared with only 5 cases where unfairness was not claimed.[6]

Clearly, it is important that U.S. producers have the opportunity to obtain relief from foreign unfair practices that cause material injury to domestic firms and workers. At the same time, however, we must remember that such relief does not come free even if it entails no U.S. public budgetary expenditures. The cost is borne in the form of higher prices paid by domestic users of the product, whether they be final consumers or firms competing in a global market and relying on the product as an essential input. Protection for one industry can result in the lessening of competitiveness in another. It is imperative, therefore, that we continue to guard against a proliferation of unfair trade actions that have no basis in rational economic principles but, instead, are proxies for outright protection.

Dumping

Dumping consists of selling a product for export below its fair value. "Less than fair value" is defined by GATT as a price below that of the like product when sold in the home market of the exporting country. In the absence of a comparable domestic price, the price at which the product is sold to third markets may be used. If neither the home market nor the third-country price is available, the standard to be used is the cost of production in the country of origin plus reasonable additions for selling cost and profit.

U.S. law is generally consistent with the GATT antidumping code but goes beyond it in specifying when and how the cost-of-production, or "constructed value," standard should be applied. Under U.S. law, the cost of production is to be used not only when home and third-country prices are unavailable but also, even when they *are* available, whenever the Secretary of Commerce "has reasonable grounds to believe or suspect" that "such sales were made at less than the cost of producing the merchandise." Under these circumstances, the Department of Commerce constructs the fair value, adding the cost of materials and fabrication plus 10 percent for overhead and general expenses plus 8 percent of total costs and expenses for profit.[7]

Increasingly, the cost of production, rather than price-to-price comparisons, is becoming the standard of choice in U.S. antidumping cases. Although official data have not been published, informal estimates suggest that 40 to 60 percent of the cases initiated since 1980 have involved comparisons between the price at which the foreign product enters the U.S. market and its cost of production in the exporting country. Moreover, the trend toward use of this constructed value has been strengthened by provisions of the Omnibus Trade and Competitiveness Act of 1988. In the section dealing with dumping by nonmarket economies, the act mandates that the Department of Commerce use constructed value as the preferred methodology in its investigations. Only if the available information for this purpose is inadequate may the department make its determination of fair value on the basis of the price of comparable products in market economies at a similar stage of economic development.

The idea that unfair pricing occurs whenever sales take place below average total cost (including overhead and profit) is economically irrational. Having sunk its investment, a firm would normally continue to operate during periods of slack demand so long as the price it receives for its product exceeds average variable rather than average total cost. The firm would thereby be covering at least some of its fixed costs for the duration of the weak market. If we applied the same antidumping standard to sales by U.S. firms, whether to the home or to foreign markets, we would be in the absurd position of regarding as objectionable sales by hundreds of American firms showing a loss for the year or anything less than an 8 percent margin of profit.

The proliferation of antidumping cases in recent years and the growing reliance on the cost-of-production standard suggest that the antidumping law as now applied has become a wide-open back door to protection.[8] What should be done about it? We suggest two changes. First, whenever verifiable prices for a like product can be obtained in either the exporting country or a third country, those prices should be the basis for comparison in determining whether sales have occurred in the United States at less than fair value. Home-market protection makes it possible for a company to maintain high prices in its domestic market and dumped prices in export markets. In such cases, the price-to-price comparison would justify the imposition of antidumping duties.

When prices for like products in the exporting country or a third country are not available, the cost of production in the exporting country should be the basis of comparison, but the relevant measure should be average variable cost rather than average total cost.* If the product is being exported for a price above the average variable cost, the allegation of unfair pricing would not be sustained. These changes would require alterations not only in U.S. law but also in the comparable provisions of GATT (Article VI) and possibly the GATT Antidumping Code of 1979 (Article 2).

There is good reason for the United States to take care in how it designs and administers its dumping law and, indeed, all its trade remedy statutes: This country's trade laws and practices are increasingly emulated by its trading partners. U.S. laws that are biased to protect the interests of U.S. producers may become the models for foreign import laws that will be used to block U.S. exports. At a time when the United States must begin to shift from a trade deficit to a trade surplus in order to finance the net foreign indebtedness we have accumulated during the 1980s, we must be particularly sensitive to protecting the interests of U.S. exporters. The United States should take the initiative in GATT to impose more discipline on national import-remedy laws to prevent the proliferation of "procedural protectionism."

Subsidies

The United States is party to both the original GATT provisions on subsidies and their later interpretation and elaboration in the 1979 Code on Subsidies and Countervailing Duties negotiated in the Tokyo Round. In 1980, the United States adopted the material-injury test for countervailing duties, bringing U.S. legislation into broad conformity with international norms on subsidies.

---

*See memorandum by W. Bruce Thomas (p. 137).

In the Uruguay Round, the U.S. objective has been to try to strengthen the code's disciplines on the use of subsidies, especially agricultural and developing-country subsidies and domestic subsidies not specifically linked to exports. Many other countries, however, have a different objective. They see the Uruguay Round primarily as an occasion to restrain what they regard as an excessive application of countervailing duties by the United States.

The United States has been by far the major initiator of countervailing duty actions. Of 460 countervailing-duty cases by all countries from 1980 to 1986, the United States accounted for 281, more than half of them against developing countries. The only other country to initiate a significant number of cases was Chile, but few of these have been sustained.[9]

What accounts for this preponderance of U.S. countervailing-duty cases? Two possible explanations can be offered. First, countries that are major subsidizers themselves may be reluctant to initiate cases against others. The extent of subsidization is far greater in other industrial countries than in the United States. According to the Organization for Economic Cooperation and Development, direct government subsidies as a percentage of gross domestic product (GDP) amounted in 1985 to 0.58 in the United States compared with 3.43 in Italy, 3.01 in France, 2.48 in Canada, 2.22 in the United Kingdom, 2.01 in Germany, and 1.15 in Japan. Moreover, the percentage has declined in the United States since 1983 while it has been on the rise in the European countries.[10] Second, other countries rely on informal and covert forms of import restrictions, involving a high degree of bureaucratic discretion, rather than on the highly transparent and formal countervailing-duty procedures.

During the entire 1980–1986 period, only one countervailing-duty action was directed against the United States. This is mainly due to the fact that most subsidized exports from the United States (and the EC as well) are agricultural products that do not cause injury to industries in the importing countries. Rather, they injure other exporting countries. This is the so-called third-country problem, in which there is no incentive for the importing country to initiate countervailing-duty action to relieve injury to a third party.

Both the GATT articles and the GATT Code on Subsidies differentiate among three types of subsidies: export subsidies on nonprimary products, export subsidies on primary products, and domestic subsidies that do not distinguish whether a product is intended for the domestic or the export market.

Export Subsidies on Nonprimary Products. The GATT treatment of trade-distorting devices reflects a basic asymmetry. Export subsidies on nonprimary products are banned, but import tariffs are permitted. Yet, both distort trade by favoring domestic over foreign production: import tariffs by granting domestic producers an artificial advantage in selling to the home market, export subsidies by granting domestic producers an artificial advantage in selling to foreign markets. Underlying the differential treatment is the implicit notion that a country has a sovereign right to defend its domestic market but not to take special measures to penetrate foreign markets—hence the historical designation of export subsidies, but not import restrictions, as an unfair trade practice.

The basic GATT rule on export subsidies is that "contracting parties shall cease to grant either directly or indirectly any form of subsidy on the export of any product, other than a primary product, which subsidy results in the sale of such product for export at a price lower than the comparable price charged for the like product in the domestic market."[11] However, in recognition of the fact that export subsidies do not necessarily imply differential pricing at home and abroad, the dual-pricing test was dropped in the 1979 code in favor of a simple prohibition of export subsidies on nonprimary products.

Although the code does not define export subsidies, it provides an illustrative list of such practices in its annex. This twelve-item list is quite comprehensive but is labeled "illustrative," presumably to leave open the possibility that practices not thought of at the time the code was drafted could be regarded as countervailable export subsidies. Two items on the list warrant special comment: the excess remission of indirect taxes on exported goods and the grant by governments of concessionary export credits.

Treatment of Indirect Taxes. The illustrative list declares the *excess* rebate of indirect taxes on exported products to be an export subsidy. By implication, this is consistent with the GATT rule that allows the rebate of *actual* indirect taxes, such as excise and value-added taxes, when goods are exported and the imposition of taxes on imports equivalent to the indirect taxes on comparable domestic goods. However, similar adjustments are not permitted for direct taxes such as corporate income taxes.

The rationale for the difference in the border treatment of the two types of taxes is that indirect taxes are assumed to be shifted forward to the consumer and are therefore reflected in the price of the product, whereas direct taxes are absorbed by producers and therefore have no effect on price. The GATT rules ensure that the producer receives equal prices for both domestic and export sales. Rebating direct taxes, however, would reduce the export price below the domestic producer price and therefore would constitute a prohibited export subsidy.

Over the years, much ink has been spilled on the question of the validity of this distinction. Some portion of direct taxes may well be shifted to consumers, and some portion of indirect taxes absorbed by producers. The extent would depend on the response of supply and demand to the imposition of the tax.

Some have argued that the present international rules place U.S. trade at a disadvantage because this country relies heavily on direct taxes that cannot be adjusted at the border, whereas Europe relies more on indirect taxes that can be adjusted, such as value-added taxes. Others reply that it is unlikely U.S. exports have been reduced or imports increased over the long run by the current practice. According to this view, on average, any initial trade-distorting effects would be offset over time by compensating changes in currency values under a regime of flexible exchange rates.

From the U.S. standpoint, however, it is unnecessary to resolve the controversial questions of the relative shiftability of direct and indirect taxes and of the extent to which any inequities in the present system tend to be offset over time by exchange rate movements. The United States would be unlikely to benefit from a change in the rules that permitted both direct and indirect taxes to be adjusted at the border.

The assumption that the United States relies more heavily on direct taxes than other industrial countries is incorrect. Social security taxes are much higher in Europe; and effective corporate income taxes abroad, although variable by country, are not on average lower than the U.S. corporate income tax (after taking deductions into account). Moreover, many small businesses are taxed at the personal rate, which is substantially higher in most other countries. Therefore, if direct taxes were rebated on exports and imposed on imports, the United States would probably not gain any net competitive advantage and might well lose.[12]

Export Credits. Although the illustrative list identifies concessionary export credits granted by governments or government-controlled institutions as export subsidies and therefore as proscribed, the code effectively withdraws GATT from implementation of this provision by acknowledging the primacy of OECD efforts to harmonize the export credit practices of its members. Accordingly, any country whose practices conform to the provisions of the OECD Agreement on Export Credits is not regarded as subsidizing its export credits.

In essence, the OECD establishes a schedule of minimum interest rates and maximum repayment periods applicable to different categories of borrowing countries defined in terms of their per capita incomes. The higher degrees of concessionality are reserved for the poorer countries. In addition, the OECD provides guidelines for disciplining the use of "mixed credits," which blend official export credits with grant aid. The guidelines identify the maximum percentage of grant aid allowed in the total package, with the higher percentages applied to the poorest countries.

U.S. exporters continue to be at a disadvantage relative to their competitors in Western Europe and Japan because of concessionary export credits. The U.S. Export-Import Bank's war chest of approximately $100 million per year is woefully inadequate to match the mixed credit resources available to exporters from other countries. Recognizing this unsatisfactory state of affairs, the Omnibus Trade and Competitiveness Act of 1988 (Section 3302) calls for a study of the tied-aid credit practices of other countries. Given U.S. budgetary constraints, however, it is doubtful that Congress would appropriate the sharply increased funds required to rectify the current imbalance of resources available for this purpose.

One way of making it easier for Congress to finance an adequately expanded war chest for matching the mixed credits offered by other countries would be to alter the budgetary treatment of the Export-Import Bank. Annual lending levels for the bank are now authorized and appropriated by Congress, and loans are treated as outlays even though defaults are rare. On the other hand, losses representing interest subsidies are not shown in the budget. C. Fred Bergsten suggests that "this budget treatment needs to be reversed, to focus on the Bank's net profits (or losses) rather than on its gross lending level to reveal real costs (if any) to the taxpayer and to avoid accounting barriers to desirable program modification."[13]

It is fundamentally irrational to grant foreign buyers more favorable credit terms than those available to domestic buyers. The ostensible justification is that concessionary export credits are a form of foreign aid. In actuality, however, the objective of outright export promotion overshadows any developmental aid considerations in the way export and mixed credit transactions are administered. The best solution for the anomaly of preferential treatment for foreign buyers is for the major trading nations to agree to an effective ban on all export credit subsidization so that no country would stand to gain an unfair advantage.

The loss of third-country markets to subsidized exports is a problem not open to solution through the usual antisubsidy remedy of countervailing duties. Such tariffs can offset unfair competition only in the importing country's home market. GATT therefore permits a country to institute antisubsidy proceedings in the third country. As a practical matter, however, this remedy is ineffective. Because third-country importers are often not competitive producers of the subsidized product (which is often agricultural), they welcome the low prices.

A reasonable remedy for the third-country subsidy problem has been put forward in the form of the countervailing subsidy. The underlying principle is that of matching other countries' subsidies. The United States has applied this remedy in the case of concessionary export credits and subsidized agricultural exports by the EC. However, the obstacle to a wider use of this technique is the budgetary costs. To meet these costs, a special duty should be imposed on imports from the subsidizing country. In order to increase the acceptability of this measure and avoid triggering a retaliatory spiral, prior authorization should be obtained from the Subsidies Committee of GATT.[14]

Export Subsidies on Primary Products. Unlike export subsidies on manufactured products, export subsidies for primary products are not banned. GATT members are simply enjoined "to seek to avoid" their use. The special treatment of agriculture with respect to the ban on export subsidies is paralleled on the import side by exceptions from the ban on import quotas.

Why have agricultural products been exempted from the international trade disciplines applying to all other products? One reason is that governments have long intervened in this sector to buffer producers from the wide fluctuations in prices and incomes to which they are subject. Even free market economies that disclaim any conscious industrial policy openly pursue activist agricultural policies. A second justification is the desire of most countries to maintain at least some measure of self-sufficiency in food for security reasons. A third reason is that farmers are well organized in most industrial countries and wield disproportionate political clout.

Although export subsidies on agricultural products are not prohibited, GATT seeks to limit their use. GATT Article XVI.3 provides that the subsidy should not be applied in a manner that results in "more than an equitable share of world export trade in that product, account being taken of the shares of the contracting parties in such trade in the product during a previous representative period, and any special factors which may have affected or may be affecting such trade in the product."

Experience has shown that this provision is so vague as to lead to endless controversy among agricultural exporting nations and particularly between the United States and the European Community. No definition is given of "equitable share" beyond the reference to export shares during a "previous representative period." But what is a representative period, and what are the "special factors" to be taken into account?

The 1979 Code on Subsidies attempts to impart greater precision to these concepts. A country would be exceeding its equitable share if the effect of the export subsidy is to displace another country's exports "bearing in mind the developments on world markets." And a previous representative period would normally be the three most recent calendar years "in which normal market conditions exist."[15] However, these passages also introduce uncertainties. If export subsidies have been in effect for a long time, the relevance of the three most recent calendar years is dubious.

A final code provision relating to primary products is that signatories agree not to grant export subsidies "in a manner which results in prices materially below those of other suppliers to the same market." However, underpricing is not generally the hallmark of export subsidization in primary products. In most cases (e.g., the EC), the purpose of the subsidy is to offset higher costs of production in protected home markets in order to allow domestic producers to meet but not necessarily undercut lower-cost competitors in foreign markets.

The need to subsidize exports of agricultural products arises primarily from costly domestic support programs[16] that not only insulate the home market from foreign competition but also generate surpluses that can only be disposed of abroad. Therefore, to deal with the root causes of the export-subsidy problem in agriculture, the domestic support programs must be addressed.

Resolving the problem of agricultural protection and support is critical to the success of the Uruguay Round. To address this problem, the United States made a sweeping proposal for a phaseout of all agricultural protection and supports by the end of the century, an idea staunchly opposed by the EC. In the meantime, however, pressure to reduce domestic government supports should be exerted by including agricultural export subsidies within the general GATT ban on export subsidies. A five-year transition period for phasing out agricultural export subsidies should be adopted.

Domestic Subsidies. Unlike export subsidies, for which reasonably established principles exist, domestic subsidies are a vast gray area. They reflect nations' differing concepts of the appropriate role of government in economic affairs. Although GATT proscribes export subsidies on nonprimary products, it permits subsidies that are not specifically related to exports. The only obligation is to try to avoid adverse effects on a country's trading partners.

The subsidies code goes even further in sanctioning domestic subsidies by explicitly recognizing their legitimacy as instruments of industrial policy. Among the objectives for which domestic subsidies may be used are: eliminating economic and social disadvantages of specific regions, facilitating the restructuring of certain industrial sectors, encouraging retraining and shifts in employment, redeploying industry for environmental reasons, and promoting research and development, especially in high-technology industries.

Examples of domestic subsidies to achieve these objectives are specified in the code: fiscal incentives, government provision of utility services or other support facilities, government subscription to equity capital, government financing of research and development, and grants, loans, or guarantees to commercial enterprises.

One reason for the tolerant treatment of domestic subsidies compared with export subsidies relates to their differing purposes. Export subsidies are designed to gain a trade advantage over competitors in foreign markets. They provide no particular incentive when domestic producers sell in the home market. In contrast, domestic subsidies provide even-handed incentives regardless of whether production is for the home or the foreign market. Therefore, there is at least a presumption that the main purpose of domestic subsidies is not to gain a trade advantage but to achieve one or more of broad social and economic objectives.

Another reason for the acceptance of domestic subsidies is the pervasiveness in modern economies of government intervention through general, sectoral, or regional aid. The interventions are often justified by the need to correct market imperfections in activities that generate external economies. For example, subsidies for research and development can compensate for the failure of the market to permit private firms to capture the full benefit of discoveries that may fall at least partly in the public domain. Regional subsidies for locating in depressed areas may compensate firms for the higher costs incurred in advancing the social objectives of reducing regional inequality. Subsidies to a particular sector, such as nonconventional energy production, may be intended to compensate domestic producers for advancing the national goal of energy independence, a contribution inadequately reflected in the market price of fuel. Subsidization of domestic economic activities is widespread in Europe and Japan, and even in the United States substantial government assistance has been rendered to high-technology sectors in conjunction with space and defense programs.

Underlying the code's treatment of domestic subsidies is the recognition that individual countries have different preferences about the role of government in their economies and that in a pluralistic world such differences should be accommodated in a manner that minimizes intrusion. In that spirit, the code acknowledges the legitimacy of domestic subsidies while recognizing their possibly adverse effects on a country's trading partners. A particular domestic subsidy of a code signatory is therefore open to challenge by another signatory on the grounds of injury to its domestic industry, nullification or impairment of benefits to which it is entitled under GATT, or other serious prejudice to its interests.

The code provides mechanisms of consultation, conciliation, and dispute settlement, including recommendations by a committee of signatories. If the committee's recommendations are not carried out, it can authorize appropriate countermeasures.

Despite what may appear to be an enlightened attempt in GATT to reconcile national industrial policies with the requirements of a liberal international trading system, the United States has been unhappy with the way the code provisions on domestic subsidies have worked out in practice. It believes they are too imprecise and rely excessively on subjective judgments about the effects of the subsidies. In the absence of effective constraints, the United States sees a self-defeating spiral of matching subsidization imposing severe financial burdens on governments and undermining the fundamental GATT principle that trade flows should reflect competitive market forces rather than government intervention. The United States has, therefore, taken the lead in the Uruguay Round in seeking to strengthen the rules on domestic subsidies.

International discipline over domestic subsidies could be strengthened in several ways. First, potentially troublesome domestic subsidies should be defined in a manner comparable to the "Illustrative List of Export Subsidies" in the present code. An example might be subsidies that exceed a specified percentage of the value of production (e.g., 5 percent) and would therefore be presumed to cause import substitution or third-country displacement, effects that could not be offset by countervailing duties. Another presumptively troublesome subsidy would be assistance to industries heavily engaged in exporting. For example, if exports account for more than 50 percent of production, a domestic subsidy would be regarded as the functional equivalent of an export subsidy. Consideration should also be given to including upstream subsidies (i.e., subsidies on inputs purchased by an industry) in cases where they result in the provision of inputs to an exporting industry at prices lower than those prevailing on world markets.

At the same time, the code should specify conditions under which subsidies would not be legally troublesome. One example would be subsidies that simply offset market imperfections in specific sectors. Another would be general or across-the-board subsidies, such as accelerated depreciation or training grants, not directed to particular industries or firms. The latter would be consistent with U.S. law, which defines an actionable domestic subsidy as one that has been bestowed on a specific enterprise or industry or group of enterprises or industries.

Second, new rules should be developed to provide more effective remedies for the adverse effects on other countries of government targeting of particular domestic industries for special assistance and support. Targeting usually entails not only subsidization of the favored, usually high-technology, industry through special credits and grants but also a coordinated government program of support including import protection during the industry's development stage and preferred government procurement.

The reason current countervailing remedies are inadequate is that the damage to competing industries in other countries may not occur for a number of years, by which time the subsidization will have become redundant and will have been withdrawn. Moreover, there may be no quantitative link, as assumed in the countervailing-duty concept, between the amount of the original subsidy and the extent of the current injury. Revisions of the GATT subsidies code are therefore needed to cope with this problem.

In formulating new rules, great caution should be exercised to minimize the possibilities of abuse. For example, many of the recent competitive pressures from Japan have arisen, not from targeting, subsidization, and home-market protection, but from other factors such as more rapid productivity growth, better quality control, the speed of commercialization of new discoveries, and the strong dollar in the first half of the 1980s. Any new rules enlarging the scope for countervailing action should therefore require demonstrations of a strong causal link between the targeted subsidies in the exporting country and the material injury in the importing country.

Because of the nature of the problem of domestic subsidies, it is not possible to lay down outright prohibitions, as in the case of export subsidies. The effects of the subsidies must be determined, and a large element of discretion and judgment is inevitable in the process. Therefore, in addition to the proposed substantive changes in the code, we welcome the agreement reached in the Uruguay Round to strengthen and streamline the GATT procedures for consultation, conciliation, and dispute settlement. Especially important is shortening the period allowed for the findings of panels and for the recommendations and decisions of the Committee on Subsidies and Countervailing Duties.

The Case of Steel

The situation in the international steel industry provides an excellent example of the multiple economic distortions that can result from a prolonged pattern of subsidization and protection. Because of steel's role as an essential material for industrial economies, few steel-producing countries are willing to allow the industry to be fully exposed to international competition. Hence, it is one of the most heavily subsidized and protected industries worldwide. Not only have producers in the older industrial countries of Europe been major recipients of government support, but many new producers have emerged in the developing countries in the form of either state-owned or state-subsidized enterprises.

Beginning in the mid-1970s, the general economic slowdown in both industrial and developing countries dampened the growth in worldwide steel demand. As a result, massive surplus capacity developed, along with intense international competition for markets. Despite these conditions, new capacity continued to come on stream into the early 1980s, in part because of construction begun before the full dimensions of the slowdown became apparent, but also because of government decisions motivated by development goals or economic nationalism. Restructuring, involving the elimination of older facilities while modernizing the remainder, proceeded unevenly. In many industrial countries, the closure of steel mills that were no longer competitive was considered politically unacceptable, especially during a period of rising unemployment.

By the early 1980s, the world steel market had become a "commercial jungle," with many nations seeking to sustain surplus steelmaking capacity by rigorously prohibiting imports while pumping their surplus into export markets at a cost of billions and sometimes tens of billions of dollars in subsidies.[17]

Confronted with this situation, the U.S. steel industry has been active in seeking import relief from foreign unfair trade practices in the form of both subsidization and dumping. To forestall dumping, the United States created a "trigger price mechanism" in 1978. Essentially, it consisted of floor prices, based on Japanese costs, below which imports of steel would automatically trigger an antidumping investigation by the U.S. government. In return, the steel industry agreed to suspend its unfair trade charges against European producers, an action that would have poisoned U.S.-European trade relations and might have jeopardized the conclusion of the Tokyo Round of multilateral trade negotiations.

The next phase in steel protection occurred in 1982, when the trigger mechanism was dropped and the industry filed massive new countervailing-duty and antidumping petitions against European producers that were operating with substantial margins of subsidization as well as dumping.[18] In order to forestall mandatory imposition of stiff import penalties, the European Community negotiated a protective market-sharing agreement with the Department of Commerce in the form of an elaborate system of quota limitations for European shipments. Not surprisingly, the U.S.-EC steel arrangement diverted trade to alternative sources, including Japan and the newly industrialized countries, which rapidly absorbed the share of the U.S. market vacated by European suppliers.

The final phase began in 1984, when, the industry, which was under intensified competition from non-European suppliers, successfully petitioned the ITC for escape-clause relief. However, instead of following the ITC recommendations, President Reagan directed the U.S. Trade Representative to negotiate voluntary restraint agreements with all significant suppliers for a period of five years. The steel industry favored this quantitative solution as a practical approach to the burgeoning steel problem, particularly in light of the rapidly appreciating dollar. The industry also wanted to include products, such as pipes and tubes, that were not covered in the ITC recommendation. Under the VRAs, steel-producing countries are today limiting their exports to the United States to approximately 20 percent of U.S. consumption. Just before the arrangement was negotiated, about 27 percent of steel sold in this country was imported.

In its quest for import relief over the years, the U.S. steel industry has emphasized unfair foreign trade practices, rightly contending that it should not be expected to compete with foreign operations that are heavily subsidized by governments. However, not all the competitive difficulties experienced by the industry have their origins in unfair practices abroad. Along with other U.S. industries in the first half of the 1980s, steel suffered from the overvalued dollar. Moreover, the industry had been slow to adopt new technologies and did not begin to close down redundant plants until the late 1970s despite the fact that consumption peaked in 1973. In addition, the U.S. domestic market has become increasingly competitive as the large integrated producers have lost market share to the minimills (smaller plants that convert steel scrap into lower-value-added finished products using modern electric furnaces and continuous casters).

The U.S. government's decision to negotiate VRAs was conditioned in part on a commitment by the U.S. steel industry to modernize its plant and equipment and to provide retraining assistance for former workers. Endeavoring to fulfill this commitment and to react to changes in the international market during the 1980s, the integrated steel industry has accomplished a good deal of restructuring and modernization. The combination of improvements in productivity, wage restraints, the closing down of outmoded plants, and the dollar's depreciation has made the U.S. industry one of the world's lowest-cost producers.[19] With the help of a comprehensive system of quantitative limits on imports, the industry has returned to profitability.

At the same time, however, the import quotas have had adverse effects on the rest of the U.S. economy. The ITC has studied this issue and has concluded that "by limiting steel imports, VRAs raise the price of steel in the U.S. market, which benefits the steel industry but raises production costs for steel-consuming industries."[20]* The quantitative dimensions of these effects may be open to dispute, but their direction is not.[21] To the extent that VRAs lead to tight supplies and higher prices, they reduce the competitiveness of U.S. manufacturers of steel-intensive products in the domestic market and impede the ability of those industries to recapture the export markets lost in the first half of the decade.

Although a negotiated solution, such as VRAs, may appear to be an effective answer to massive trade problems that threaten broader international relationships, voluntary export restraints are a particularly undesirable form of protection. Unlike tariffs, they rigidify the pattern of trade by fixing the market share of foreign suppliers in a situation of changing comparative advantage. For example, under existing VRAs, Korea, which is one of the world's most efficient steel producers, has a smaller share of the U.S. market than it would under open competition; but Brazil, a chronically high-cost producer, has a guaranteed share in a market in which it would never be able to compete under an open system. Moreover, to the extent that there is a difference between the protected U.S. price and the world market price of U.S. imports, it accrues mainly to the foreign exporter in the form of quota rents rather than to the U.S. Treasury in the form of import duties. Finally, the elaborate system of quantitative import controls in steel undermines U.S. efforts to strengthen GATT and reduces our bargaining power in negotiating to get rid of other countries' restrictions in sectors where the United States is competitive, such as agriculture and services.

In July 1989, the Bush administration extended the VRAs for two and a half years. During this period, the Office of the U.S. Trade Representative will endeavor to negotiate an international consensus to remove the unfair trade practices that gave rise to the VRAs.

The extension will also allow more time for U.S. steel companies to adjust and modernize in order to sustain profitability. Although the U.S. steel industry is currently cost-competitive, it has lagged in the modernization of outmoded plant and equipment. During the industry's years of unprofitable performance, U.S. private companies (especially

---

*See memorandum by W. Bruce Thomas (p. 138).

integrated producers) have not been able to attract capital or generate sufficient internal cash flow to prevent a net disinvestment. Meanwhile, overseas, where massive infusions of public capital have displaced private capital, foreign producers have been able to keep abreast of the latest technology.[22] The impact of this is evident in the fact that only 60 percent of U.S. output is produced by continuous casting, compared with 95 percent in Japan, 80 percent in Europe, and 75 percent in South Korea and Taiwan.[23]

Although these problems warrant attention, there is evidence that the burden of financing huge subsidy costs is inclining at least some foreign countries to move away from past policies of support for their steel industries. For example, Australia has abandoned its steel subsidy program, and British Steel has been privatized. U.S. policy should encourage that trend at what may be an important juncture in the direction of steel policy around the world.

We therefore strongly support the U.S. government's decision to seek an international consensus on steel trade policy that would provide effective disciplines over government aid and intervention in the steel sector and would lower barriers to global trade in steel. We also concur with the decision to enforce vigorously the laws against injurious dumping and subsidization after the VRAs are lifted in 1992. The normal remedies for these unfair practices are offsetting tariffs, which are far superior to rigid quotas for the regions cited above.

In order to prevent an onslaught of arbitrary antidumping actions, we favor prompt enactment of the revisions we proposed earlier in the criteria for determining the existence of dumping: primary reliance on price comparisons, with cost analyses only a fallback resort. In the latter case, average variable rather than average total costs should serve as the criterion. The standard of average total costs, including an 8 percent profit margin, is untenable for an industry such as steel with high overhead costs and a cyclical pattern of demand. In slack times, steel producers everywhere will, in practice, accept prices that cover variable, but not total, costs.

At the same time, the United States should press in GATT for the opening of the exporting countries' own steel markets. Exposing those countries to the threat of import competition would discourage the practice of covering fixed costs by high domestic prices and then exporting at prices based on variable cost.

Unfair Restrictions on Access to Foreign Markets

During the 1980s, the emphasis of U.S. trade policy has shifted from combating *unfair imports* through antidumping and countervailing duties to an aggressive pursuit of more open foreign markets for American exporters. The statutory basis for the drive against *unfair export restrictions* is Section 301 of the Trade Act of 1974.

Concern about restrictions on U.S. access to foreign markets is not new. Forerunners to Section 301 can be found in the tariff acts of 1890, 1897, and 1909, which authorized the President to levy tariffs on certain imports if, in his judgment, the foreign country imposed duties or other restrictions that he deemed unreasonable or unjust.

Section 301 gives the administration broad powers to act against practices determined *unilaterally* to be unjustifiable, unreasonable, or discriminatory. "Unjustifiable" foreign practices are those in violation of the international legal rights of the United States. "Unreasonable" acts are defined to include practices that are not necessarily in violation of U.S. rights but that are nonetheless deemed "unfair and inequitable," such as export targeting or denial of worker rights. "Discriminatory" implies the denial of national or most-favored-nation treatment for U.S. goods, services, or investment.

The principal weapon authorized by Section 301 for attacking these unfair trade practices is retaliation or the threat of retaliation in the form of restrictions on access to the U.S. market. The retaliatory features of Section 301 were strengthened by Congress in the so-called Super 301 provisions of the Omnibus Trade and Competitiveness Act of 1988.

The revised statute builds on the annual report of the Office of the U.S. Trade Representative on foreign trade barriers affecting goods, services, investment, and intellectual property protection whether or not the barriers are consistent with international trade rules.[24] It requires the U.S. Trade Representative to identify "priority practices" that, if eliminated, could significantly increase U.S. exports. It also requires the identification of "priority countries" where significant trade barriers are pervasive. After identifying these priority practices and countries, the U.S. Trade Representative must initiate investigations and seek to negotiate agreements to discontinue the practices within 12 to 18 months. If an agreement is not reached, the Trade Representative must determine whether the practice under investigation is unjustifiable, unreasonable, or discriminatory and therefore actionable under Section 301. If the practice is deemed unfair in this sense, the Trade Representative must determine what retaliatory action, if any, should be taken.

Because of the way the amendments to Section 301 are written in the Omnibus Trade Act, it is often assumed that retaliation is mandatory in the case of unjustifiable foreign trade practices (i.e., those in violation of international agreements), in contrast with the discretionary nature of the authority to retaliate in cases of unreasonable or discriminatory practices. Actually, there are a number of exceptions to mandatory retaliation based, inter alia, on a Presidential determination of serious harm to the national security and a disproportionate impact on the national economy.

In May 1989, the Office of the U.S. Trade Representative released its first list of priority practices and priority countries. Japan was cited for technical barriers to trade in forest products and government procurement restrictions on satellites and supercomputers. Brazil was singled out for quantitative import quotas and restrictive licensing regimes that inhibit imports of manufactured and agricultural products. India was cited for trade-related investment restrictions and barriers to trade in services.[25]

Although a great deal of controversy surrounded these designations, they are not inconsistent with other recent trade policy actions. Between September 7, 1985, and June 15, 1988, the United States challenged unfair trade practices twenty-six times by expediting, initiating, or threatening to initiate Section 301 investigations. A number of investigations were initiated by the administration rather than by private petition, and three resulted in retaliation.[26] The cases involved a diversity of countries and products, including beer and wine from Taiwan, semiconductors from Japan, cigarettes from Korea, informatics from Brazil, citrus and almonds from the EC, soybeans from Argentina, and almonds from India.

The basic idea behind Section 301 is the perfectly reasonable principle that the United States should use access to its vast domestic market as a bargaining tool to open markets abroad, an action that often benefits exporters not only in the United States but in other countries as well. Indeed, the principle of reciprocity underlies the eight rounds of multilateral negotiations to liberalize trade in which the United States has played a leadership role. However, the way in which the principle is applied in Section 301 departs sharply from the traditional conduct of liberal trade.

The unilateral character of Super 301 is both its main deficiency and its inherent danger. It can be used to attack foreign practices that are not illegal under our international agreements but that are unilaterally deemed to be "unreasonable," defined in U.S. law as unfair and inequitable. Clearly, opinions differ on whether a particular practice is unfair. A Japanese view of the process was recently expressed by a former Vice Minister of International Trade and Industry: "The U.S. uses its own criteria to determine unfairness, prosecutes the case itself, and hands down the sentence."[27] However, the U.S. position, especially in regard to Japan, is that certain government and industry practices may not be formally illegal under GATT but are nevertheless unfair because they are contrary to the spirit of that agreement. In our view, these are best dealt with by a strong combination of business-to-business and government-to-government negotiations, as outlined in *Strengthening U.S.-Japan Economic Relations: An Action Program for the Public and Private Sectors,* a 1989 joint statement by CED and its Japanese counterpart organization, Keizai Doyukai.

Section 301 may be regarded as unilateral in a second sense. It attempts to remove a foreign trade restriction, which may be entirely legal, without any equivalent U.S. concession. This is inconsistent with the traditional notion of liberalizing trade through mutual rather than unilateral concessions.

The idea of reciprocity in the sense of roughly equal market access lies behind many of the recent changes in U.S. trade law. But it is a different concept of reciprocity from that of equivalent *increases* in access at the margin, which has served as the basis for past progress in liberalizing world trade. As espoused by the United States and applied in GATT, reciprocity meant a broad balance between the reduction in trade barriers offered by the United States and the liberalization obtained collectively from other major trading partners in multilateral negotiations.

This traditional concept of reciprocity had three distinguishing features: First, it applied to the results of the negotiations as a whole rather than to individual products, industries, or sectors. Second, it was multilateral rather than country-by-country in its approach. Third, it was applied in a way that could lead only to reductions of trade barriers, not to increases. To the extent that offers of reductions could not be broadly matched by other participants, the scope of the liberalization was limited, but the result was not an increase in trade restrictions. With this bias toward opening markets, the principle of reciprocity became a driving force for trade liberalization under American leadership.

Although the Bush administration insists that Super 301 actions will not undermine multilateral efforts at trade liberalization, the notion of reciprocity underlying recent trade policy and legislation departs from all three elements of the original conception. First, it has a distinct sectoral focus, calling for symmetrical treatment in individual product sectors, as illustrated most explicitly in the telecommunications provision of the Omnibus Trade Act.[28] Second, it seeks to force equivalence in external trading opportunities in a bilateral rather than a multilateral context. Third, the new policy is carried out on the basis of threats of retaliation in the form of *increases* in U.S. trade barriers when this country unilaterally determines that the balance is unfair. Given the Super 301 requirements of the Omnibus Trade Act, however, the administration has thus far applied the statute with commendable discretion.

Trade restrictions that are deemed unfair are not a unique problem faced by U.S. exporters. European Community exporters claim that they face similar problems when trading with the United States. Recently, the EC issued an extensive report on significant U.S. trade barriers, including some of questionable consistency with U.S. international obligations.[29] Similarly, developing countries have pointed to U.S. bilateral restraints under the Multifiber Agreement as inconsistent with GATT principles.

Nevertheless, the threat of retaliation through denial of access to the huge U.S. market can occasionally serve as an effective strategy to open foreign markets and to protect U.S. interests under international trade agreements. Used sparingly, bilateral pressure is not necessarily inconsistent with advancing the objectives of a multilateral trading system. In some cases it may provide the foreign government with the rationale for overcoming domestic political opposition to specific measures of trade liberalization that add to the long-run benefit of its economy as a whole.

At the same time, we must not lose sight of the dangers inherent in an aggressive use of threats of retaliation under Section 301. When negotiations pursued under Section 301 lead to improved access to foreign markets for U.S. exports, Section 301 has succeeded. When negotiations do not lead to improved access and the United States retaliates, Section 301 has failed. Retaliation does not solve the problem of the U.S. exporter, and by restricting access of foreign goods to the U.S. market, it harms the U.S. economy as well as the foreign exporter. As Adam Smith noted more than 200 years ago: "There may be good policy in retaliations . . . when there is a probability that they will procure the repeal of high duties or prohibitions complained of. . . . When there is no probability that any such repeal can be procured, it seems a bad method of compensating the injury done to certain classes of people, to do another injury to ourselves. . . ."[30]

An additional risk is that retaliation can escalate into a cycle of counterretaliation, as was imminent following the recent Section 301 action against the EC on hormone-treated beef.[31] Although retaliation can be effective as a measured response to egregious foreign practices that impede U.S. trade, widespread resort to this weapon could lead to the mutual unraveling of past gains in opening markets to the detriment of all trading nations.

Beyond these important concerns of shooting ourselves in the foot and risking counterretaliation, there lies another, very important consideration. For the past fifty years, the United States has led the world in building a system of international law governing trade in which people act according to rules. We have not succeeded as well as we would have liked, but we have made great progress, and the process of building that system continues today. If we now begin to abandon that effort by relying on unilateral judgments of others' actions, we will set a quite different example for the world to emulate. If, as a result, other countries begin to make demands upon their trading partners to change laws and practices that are *not* inconsistent with international rules by threatening and carrying out retaliation, rather than by offering concessions, the result would be chaos.

An excessively aggressive U.S. trade policy will undermine this country's long-term interest in building a stronger system of international rules. We should be aggressive to defend and promote U.S. interests. At the same time, we should be cautious and deliberate in the measures we adopt, acting not out of frustration and anger in ways that will thwart our long-term objectives but rather in ways calculated to achieve them.

Finally, as the Bush administration and many observers in and out of government recognize, the "trade deficit [which provided the original political rationale for Super 301] is not the product of trade barriers."[32] There is no evidence that *increasing* restrictions abroad can explain a significant part of the $130 billion rise in the U.S. trade deficit during the 1980s.

A recent study, based on World Bank and GATT data, attempts to quantify the extent of *hard-core* nontariff measures, a category of restrictions closely identified with unfair trade practices.[33] Hard-core barriers include import prohibitions, quantitative restrictions, voluntary export restraints, variable levies, Multifiber Agreement restrictions, and nonautomatic licensing of imports. (Excluded are such measures as health and safety requirements and technical standards.) The study shows that the proportion of imports subject to hardcore restrictions in 1986 was slightly higher in the United States than in the European Community and was by far the highest in Japan. However, the *increase* in the proportions between 1981 and 1986 was greatest in the United States (from 11 to 16 percent). The comparable figures for the EC were 12 and 15 percent, and for Japan the proportion was 25 percent in both years. The study concludes that new hard-core import restrictions imposed by other industrial countries in the 1980s may have cost the United States about $6 billion in 1986 but that similar restrictions imposed by this country may have reduced U.S. imports by $17 billion. In short, it is unlikely that the U.S. trade balance was adversely affected by new nontariff barriers in the 1980s.[34]

In interpreting these results, two serious limitations of such efforts at quantification should be borne in mind. First, the calculations of the extent of nontariff barriers in each country are based on the proportion of its imports subject to the restrictions without regard to the severity of the individual restrictions.[35] Second, the calculations take into account only formal and official measures, ignoring informal barriers (such as administrative guidance) and unofficial restrictions (such as those resulting from the practices of industry groups). Informal and unofficial restrictions are minimal in the United States compared with those in Japan and most other countries.

How can unfair restrictions on access to foreign markets be dealt with in a way that maximizes the chances for effective redress while minimizing the need to resort to unilateral retaliation? We believe the answer lies in channeling as many cases as possible to the improved multilateral GATT dispute settlement facility on which a consensus has now been reached in the Uruguay Round.

In the past, many countries have grown frustrated with GATT dispute settlement procedures based on consensus and voluntary compliance. Although the process has been successful in many cases, it has not proved satisfactory in others. As one of the first concrete achievements of the Uruguay negotiations, agreement has been reached on measures to streamline the process through improvements such as time limits on stages in the process; steps to encourage use of mediation; provision for the alternative of a speedy, flexible arbitration mechanism; and the automatic right to a special panel to consider and report on a case unless the GATT council decides otherwise. Resolving disputes among members fairly and expeditiously should be one of GATT's central roles. The United States should take the lead in enhancing its effectiveness in this role so that individual members will have less cause to resort to unilateral action.

Although the United States has been a principal *demandeur* for a more effective GATT dispute-settlement mechanism, its behavior has led others to question the sincerity of our commitment. For example, for almost a year the United States delayed before adopting a GATT panel report that found aspects of Section 337 of U.S. trade law (dealing mainly with patent and trademark infringements) to be in violation of GATT. Moreover, even when the United States has accepted panel reports that ruled against us (as in the cases of the customs user fee, the Superfund tax, and the sugar quota program), Congress has failed to change the law to bring the United States into conformity with its obligations. Leadership requires action by example as well as by exhortation. If the United States wants a more effective GATT dispute-settlement mechanism—and we strongly believe that such a mechanism is in the U.S. interest—it will have to show more good faith by accepting the results of the process.

We have one final suggestion about Section 301. Its purpose is to improve U.S. access to foreign markets, not to reduce foreign access to the U.S. market. Therefore, in applying Section 301, there should be no presumption that retaliatory action would necessarily take the form of restrictions on imports of the same product or service category as that for which the petitioner is seeking to open a market abroad. This would tend to reduce the temptation to use Section 301 as a back-door way of winning protection in the U.S. market. The proper route for seeking relief from seriously injurious import competition is Section 201 of our trade law.

Intellectual Property Rights

The protection of intellectual property rights (IPRs) is a matter of highest priority for the United States and must become a central aspect of U.S. trade policy.

The production of and trade in counterfeit and pirated goods is rapidly increasing. It is no longer just the infringement of well-known trademarks for consumer goods such as Levi's, Lacoste, and Louis Vuitton. The problem has spread to more sophisticated products such as computer software, audiovisual goods, pharmaceuticals, and other high-technology products. Unless widespread violations are checked, investment in research and development will be discouraged and the pace of world development slowed.

Inadequate protection of intellectual property is an unfair practice that entails three types of trade distortions: It displaces sales of legitimate goods in the domestic market; it decreases exports to, foreign sales in, and royalties from the countries that abuse intellectual property; and it shrinks the market for legitimate goods in third countries.

Losses from the misappropriation of IPRs are enormous. The U.S. economy, like those of Japan and many Western European countries, includes a growing number of knowledge-based industries dependent on large investments in research and development. For these industries, the key expense is no longer the cost of production but the cost of innovation, which must be recouped from sales in volume both at home and abroad. For example, it takes an average of ten years and $125 million to bring a new pharmaceutical product to market. Yet, if not legally prevented, a chemist could produce the drug in sufficient quantities to make it unprofitable for the legitimate producer. A new family of integrated circuits costs $150 million or more to design, but the same chips can be copied for less than $1 million. A copy of a $500

U.S. software program can be bought in the Far East for $7.50. According to an ITC estimate, worldwide losses to U.S. industry in 1986 from foreign infringement of intellectual property rights ranged upwards of $43 billion.[36]

IPRs are granted through national legal systems and therefore apply to particular countries. Trade distortions can thus arise from activities that are legal in countries providing lower levels of protection for such rights than are the norm in the industrialized nations. For example, some countries do not extend protection to pharmaceuticals or to the newer technologies such as software and semiconductor chips. Under these circumstances, the principle of national treatment, which is included in all international conventions on IPRs, is clearly not enough. It may prevent discrimination against foreigners, but it does not address the main problem of weak national legislation and enforcement.

The United States has a unilateral defense against IPR violations when they involve products imported into this country. Under Section 337 of the Tariff Act of 1930, the ITC is authorized to investigate allegations of such unfair practices and to exclude the imports in question. Prior to the enactment of the Omnibus Trade and Competitiveness Act of 1988, the complainant had to show injury, but that requirement has now been eliminated in certain IPR cases. A large proportion of the ITC's docket has consisted of intellectual property cases under Section 337. We would expect an even greater flow of petitions for relief in the future.

In addition, the United States has engaged in a major campaign to improve foreign practices affecting its IPRs abroad. It has included intellectual property criteria in the Caribbean Basin Initiative and the General System of Preferences for developing countries. In its bilateral efforts, the U.S. hand has been strengthened by the 1984 trade law amendments that identified inadequate intellectual property laws of U.S. trading partners as constituting a basis for retaliatory action under Section 301. But the main current weapon for exerting pressure on foreign countries is the so-called Special 301 intellectual property provisions of the Omnibus Trade and Competitiveness Act of 1988.

The Special 301 authority is designed to enhance U.S. ability to negotiate improvements in foreign intellectual property regimes through bilateral initiatives that carry in the background the threat of retaliation in the form of restrictions on access to the U.S. market. The statute requires the Office of the U.S. Trade Representative to identify those foreign countries denying protection of IPRs and market access to U.S. firms relying on such protection and to determine which of those countries are "priority countries" triggering an accelerated six-month investigation. However, where countries are making significant progress in negotiations, the Trade Representative is precluded from designating them as priority countries.

Because of progress made in various negotiations, the Trade Representative has identified no priority countries under Special 301. Instead, it has named twenty-five countries whose practices deserve special attention. Of these, eight have been placed on a "priority watch list": Brazil, India, Mexico, People's Republic of China, South Korea, Saudi Arabia, Taiwan, and Thailand. Accelerated action plans for improving intellectual property protection are being pursued with each of the countries.

U.S. bilateral efforts have already achieved significant improvements in intellectual property protection. Recent examples include the commitment of China to provide copyright protection for computer software, the resolution by Colombia of the royalty remission problem in motion pictures, the adoption by Saudi Arabia of a patent law, the establishment by Korea of an enforcement task force for intellectual property, and the introduction by Japan of an accelerated examination and appeals procedure.[37]

However, bilateral efforts to deal with the IPR problem are strictly a second-best approach. They are generally based on coercion through threats of retaliation by the stronger party rather than on consensus. Moreover, they raise the danger that benefits will be limited to the partner involved, thereby discriminating against outsiders. In addition, multilateral approaches through existing international treaties—the Berne Convention and the Universal Copyright Convention for copyrights and the Paris Convention for patents and trademarks—have serious gaps in coverage and deficiencies in standards. Most important, they do not provide dispute-settlement facilities or effective enforcement mechanisms.

Because of these deficiencies, we strongly endorse the lead taken by the United States in the Uruguay Round to develop a comprehensive GATT agreement on improved and modernized standards for the protection of intellectual property rights and effective procedures and facilities for enforcement and dispute settlement. Previous GATT negotiations on this subject were more narrowly focused on a trademark anticounterfeiting code enforceable at the border. Although some developing countries would like to limit the present negotiations to an anticounterfeiting code, we believe that would be a mistake. Such a code would essentially be a border control device to intercept the importation of goods bearing counterfeit trademarks. It would not deal with piracy, counterfeiting, and infringement at the source. We therefore strongly favor an agreement that comprehends all intellectual property and provides for nonborder enforcement as well.

   The principal obstacle to more rapid progress on IPRs in the current round of negotiations is the attitude of some of the developing countries, most notably Brazil and India. Behind their opposition lies an ideology that regards technological innovation as a public rather than a private capital good. As in the case of other public goods, the use of technology by one party does not deprive any other party of its use. Therefore, according to this view, payment should not be exacted for its use, and the attempt to do so through an IPR system is simply technological imperialism.

   Implicit in this line of reasoning is the premise that technology is a stock for which the investment has already been sunk rather than a flow for which huge new expenditures are constantly required. In the absence of adequate payment for the use of technology, the flow would dry up.

   As the GATT negotiations have proceeded, more and more developing countries have joined the ranks of those supporting a comprehensive agreement. Many realize the importance of rewarding invention as a stimulus to technological innovation, particularly as they themselves are now on the threshold of becoming creators of valuable intellectual property. And there is a growing appreciation that the willingness of companies in the developed world to transfer technology and invest capital in developing countries is greatly affected by the status of protection for intellectual property.

   We cannot emphasize too strongly our conviction that it is in the interest of the developing as well as the developed countries to strengthen the international regime for the protection of IPRs. It would be undesirable for the United States and other countries already committed to negotiating a comprehensive agreement to water down the provisions in order to attract a greater number of those who hesitate or are opposed. We are confident that most of the latter nations will eventually find it in their interest to join.

Competitive Disadvantages Contained
in U.S. Law and Regulation

   From a U.S. perspective, unfair trade practices normally refer to actions by foreign companies or governments that reduce the international competitiveness of U.S. products or services in violation of the letter or spirit of international law. However, a number of serious impediments to the ability of U.S firms to compete in the international marketplace stem from *domestic* laws and regulations. In effect, self-inflicted disadvantages can be considered unfair trade practices. Such disadvantages are found in a number of areas including strategic export controls, antitrust law, the Foreign Corrupt Practices Act, product liability law, environmental regulations, and tax legislation. In each field, we believe that reforms would improve U.S. international competitiveness.

Strategic Export Controls*

Since the early post-World War II period, the United States and its allies have tried to maintain tight controls on trade with Communist regimes by limiting their access to the critical products and technologies underlying the defense of the West. With this objective in mind, the Coordinating Committee on Multilateral Export Controls (COCOM) was established in 1949. Despite numerous multilateral initiatives, however, COCOM members have never been able to agree unanimously on a list of restricted products, and the enforcement of agreed controls has been uneven. Within COCOM, the United States has been the most vigorous about enforcement. It also maintains several bilateral agreements with non-COCOM countries on export controls and imposes unilateral restrictions on products not covered by any international agreement.

Despite its obvious flaws, this system of export restrictions has succeeded in keeping some strategically sensitive technologies out of Communist countries. But with the globalization of production and markets and the rapid dissemination of technology to non-COCOM countries, stemming the flow of advanced technology to Communist countries has become much more difficult.

Newly industrialized countries such as Taiwan and South Korea are now major participants in the manufacturing and assembly operations of high-technology industries. As non-COCOM countries intent on increasing exports, they sell freely to both the People's Republic of China and the Soviet bloc. Hence, even if there were perfect consensus within COCOM on appropriate controls, it would be difficult to prevent Communist governments completely from acquiring strategically significant technologies.

The pace of technological innovation itself also undermines the effective functioning of controls. It is almost impossible for policy makers to keep up with the new developments and to maintain controls that are consistent with changing realities.

A 1987 study by the National Academy of Sciences summarized the major problems with U.S. export controls and their detrimental effects on U.S. competitiveness:

---

*See memorandum by John Diebold (p. 139).

The scope of current U.S. export controls encompasses too many products and technologies to be administered effectively. In particular, the U.S. government has not provided a justification for the continued control of low-level technologies—such as those technologies which are available from foreign sources with little or no restrictions.

Foreign customers are discouraged from relying on U.S. suppliers because of uncertainties about future license approvals, follow-on service, availability of parts and components, and possible re-export prohibitions.

Delays in the licensing process or uncertainty about obtaining an applicable export license often result in lost export sales.

U.S. producers, especially small- to medium-sized firms, are deterred from exporting by the complexities and delays of the export control regulations.

From a global perspective, some aspects of the U.S. export controls (particularly re-export controls) are also seen as conflicting with widely accepted principles of international law and national sovereignty. The extraterritorial aspects of U.S. export controls tend to create mistrust among U.S. allies as well as resentment against U.S. policy. As a consequence, the legal justifications of U.S. export controls have been weakened, and foreign compliance with U.S. restrictions has become less than satisfactory.[38]

Because high-technology industries relying heavily on research and development are vital to U.S. competitiveness, the long-term economic consequences of a marked shift of advantage away from the United States could be far-reaching. The continuation of controls on exports that are readily available from alternative suppliers could result in a downward spiral of shrinking markets, curtailed production, and ultimately damaging disinvestment. In some critical industries, such as semiconductors and computer systems, there are significant economies of scale in production. Therefore, policies that close off substantial markets raise the unit costs of American producers, placing them at a severe disadvantage relative to unconstrained foreign suppliers. Lower sales, in turn, are likely to lead to subsequent reductions in research and development expenditures and the investment required to bring innovations to market quickly.

Reacting to the mounting problems, Congress revised the law on strategic export controls in the 1988 Omnibus Trade and Competitiveness Act. The new law removes controls on certain low-technology items that are easy for controlled countries to acquire elsewhere. It also stipulates that unilateral controls will be of limited duration. On all controlled items, foreign availability will be reviewed on a continuous basis, and the list of controlled products will be updated quarterly. The list of militarily critical items will be updated on an ongoing basis. Re-export licenses will no longer be required when the value of the controlled content is 25 percent or less of the total value of the foreign goods in which the parts are incorporated. Re-export authority is still required for items that the Secretary of Commerce deems to be highly critical technology. The decision as to what is highly critical will rest with the Department of Commerce.

The act also directs the National Academy of Sciences to conduct a comprehensive study of the adequacy of the current export administration system in safeguarding national security while maintaining international competitiveness and Western technological preeminence. The objectives of the study are (1) to identify the existing goods and technologies that are likely to make a crucial difference to the military capabilities of controlled countries and which of those goods are available from other sources, (2) to develop criteria to define additional goods to be subject to control, (3) to demonstrate how to apply the criteria to the control list, (4) to develop ways to improve U.S. and multilateral assessments of foreign availability, and (5) to develop proposals to improve the administration of the export-control program, including procedures to ensure timely, predictable, and effective decision making.

Recognizing that computers are often at the heart of export-control problems and that computer technology is increasingly difficult to control, the academy has already made a number of recommendations specific to the computer industry.

CED strongly endorses the steps taken in the trade act. However, we recommend a further improvement in the form of U.S. sunset laws. All of our COCOM restrictions should carry an expiration date; when that date is reached, the authorities could reconsider the necessity of the restriction and conclude whether or not to extend it.

Additional improvements can be sought within COCOM. Multilateral discussions in COCOM in 1988 resulted in the removal of a considerable number of semiconductor and computer products from both the U.S. and the COCOM lists. Member countries should continue to review the specific list of excluded items. Higher walls around a narrower set of technologies would be both more effective and more enforceable and would provide the basis for greater cohesion within COCOM. A successful multilateral effort will foster fairer trade by allowing market forces rather than differences in national export controls to determine the global competitiveness of U.S. firms.

Economic Sanctions

Strategic export controls under the aegis of COCOM are only one form of economic sanction affecting the international flow of goods and services. Throughout history, governments have deliberately suspended normal trade or financial relations as a means to coerce other states to adopt policies they favor or to reverse a course of action they oppose. The underlying assumption is that economic deprivation, applied either generally or to a critical economic sector, will achieve the desired effect, enabling the government to demonstrate the power of its convictions without resorting to military action.

Since World War I, the United States has been the dominant user of economic sanctions for foreign policy objectives. One study documents ninety-nine cases of economic sanctions between 1918 and 1983, sixty-two of which were initiated with varying degrees of success by the United States.[39]

The U.S. law most frequently used as a basis for sanctions is the Export Administration Act, originally passed in 1949 to establish strategic export controls but amended on numerous subsequent occasions. The stated purposes of export controls include the protection of national security, the furtherance of U.S. foreign policy interests, and the safeguarding of commodities in short supply.

In 1979, President Carter used this authority to embargo the export of grain to the Soviet Union after the 1979 Soviet invasion of Afghanistan. President Reagan used it in 1981–1983, following the imposition of martial law in Poland, to embargo sales by U.S. firms and their foreign subsidiaries of oil and gas transmission and refining technology for use by the Soviet Union on its natural gas pipeline to Western Europe.[40] The latter action was made possible by the expanded authority in the 1977 amendments to the Export Administration Act which authorized the control of goods and technology exported by any person subject to the jurisdiction of the United States. The new authority permitted the Department of Commerce to exercise control over foreign-origin goods and technological data re-exported by U.S.-owned or U.S.-controlled companies.[41]

Authorization for economic sanctions against specific countries is contained in a variety of other single-purpose laws. For example, the Foreign Assistance Act of 1961 expressly bans trade with Cuba. Elements of the Tax Reform Act of 1976 coupled with 1977 amendments to the Export Administration Act are designed to discourage cooperation with international boycotts not endorsed by the U.S. government, such as the Arab boycott of Israel. The International Security and Development Cooperation Act of 1985 prohibits imports from and exports to Libya and bans imports of goods and services from countries supporting terrorism. In an attempt to end human rights abuse in South Africa, the Comprehensive Anti-Apartheid Act of 1986 bars all trade and financial transactions with that country.

Ironically, as U.S. reliance on economic sanctions as a foreign policy tool has increased, their effectiveness has diminished. The internationalization of the world economy has dramatically expanded trading options for all countries, thereby reducing the opportunities for sanctions to succeed even when they are employed by as big a trading country as the United States. To achieve a major and lasting impact with unilateral sanctions, the country imposing them must hold a near monopoly on trade with the targeted country or stand as the exclusive supplier of an economically critical commodity. Alternatively, the sanction-imposer must achieve a high degree of cooperation among its allies. In the majority of cases, the interests of allied countries tend not to coincide to the extent required to ensure an effective response. The difficulty of achieving a consensus within COCOM is evidence of this diversity of priorities.

In an interdependent global economy, poorly conceived sanctions may not only fail to achieve their policy objective but may also cause more harm domestically than abroad. Even sanctions of short duration can create lasting competitive disadvantages for domestic firms engaged in international trade. The interruption of trade and financial contacts can erode a firm's reputation for reliability. Once customers switch suppliers, they may not be inclined to risk resuming trade even after political relations improve. In light of this situation, CED urges policy makers, when contemplating the use of sanctions, to undertake a thorough assessment of the potential for success as well as the likely costs to our own economy and trade position. The result should be a more judicious use of sanctions and greater credibility to the policies they are intended to serve.

U.S. Antitrust Law

In today's highly integrated world economy, the opportunities for anticompetitive behavior are reduced by the existence of large numbers of strong firms competing in linked global markets. U.S. antitrust law, as applied both domestically and extraterritorially, has therefore come into question as possibly inhibiting the international competitiveness of U.S. industries.

The burden of U.S. antitrust law and similarly motivated statutes, such as the Glass-Steagall Act, is borne by American companies competing internationally in both manufacturing and financial services.

Financial Services. In the financial industry, U.S. banking regulations, originally designed to prevent undue concentration of economic power, to promote domestic competition, and to preserve the viability of small financial institutions around the country, now impede the international competitiveness of American institutions.

Whereas universal banking, which permits full integration of securities and banking activities, is becoming commonplace in both Japan and Europe, U.S. law (the Glass-Steagall Act and the Bank Holding Company Act) continues to restrict such integration. By gaining the economies of scale resulting from the integration of similar functions and the provision of a broader range of services, foreign institutions have taken the lead in international banking. In terms of asset size, only one American commercial bank ranks among the top thirty internationally.

Moreover, EC directives for 1992, which touch on virtually every aspect of financial services, have given impetus to many nations to restructure their financial systems for greater efficiency and international competitiveness. Both Canada and the United Kingdom have recently completed significant restructuring, and further changes are on the horizon in Japan and Switzerland.

In this country, too, the law needs to be overhauled to reflect the worldwide nature of the financial services industry. In our view, it should be possible to remove the inefficiencies in our domestic financial system that are crippling U.S. firms internationally without weakening the government's prudential oversight function. Also, strict functional separation of banking, securities, and insurance need not be the mechanism by which the government prevents anticompetitive behavior. Adequate safeguards against market concentration already exist in the antitrust statutes applied to all industrial sectors.*

Joint Ventures. Antitrust concerns have also intensified in high-technology industries. Because the costs of developing advanced technologies and bringing them rapidly to market often exceed the resources of any single firm, cooperative ventures among potentially competing firms in research and development as well as in production are becoming more attractive to U.S. business. Such joint activities are relatively common in Europe and Japan. They are also generally legal in the United States as long as they do not lead to arrangements that restrict sales or raise prices of the product or service for U.S. users. However, U.S. firms have traditionally been reluctant to pursue such options for fear of antitrust suits seeking treble damages.

---

*See memorandum by Robert C. Winters (p. 139).

To address this problem, Congress passed the National Cooperative Research Act (NCRA) in 1984. Under NCRA, joint-venture participants engaged in research and development must provide advance notice of their activities to the Justice Department and the Federal Trade Commission. After doing so, the joint venture may still be sued under the antitrust laws, but only for actual rather than treble damages. Further, the statute requires that the rule of reason, not the *per se* rule, be used to analyze the effects of such joint research and development ventures, whether or not antitrust officials are notified in advance. Under the rule of reason, if there are more procompetitive benefits than anticompetitive effects, then the arrangement does not violate antitrust laws.

Prompted by the significant erosion of U.S. international competitiveness in semiconductors, several bills have been introduced in both the Senate and the House of Representatives to extend antitrust reforms to joint manufacturing. Two basic approaches have been proposed: One merely extends the advance notice and other features of the NCRA to manufacturing activities. The other would adopt certification procedures similar to those provided in the Export Trading Company Act of 1982 and apply them to joint manufacturing ventures. A certificate would be granted after the Departments of Commerce and Justice reviewed the application and determined that the joint-venture arrangements would not threaten competition. Certification would be renewed periodically following reviews by the government to ensure that the venture had not evolved in a way that restrained competition.

CED believes that as a general principle whatever liberalized treatment is provided for joint ventures engaged in the production of goods should also be provided for those involved in the provision of services. This would be consistent with the Export Trading Company Act, which encourages the formation and operation of export trade associations and companies in both the goods and the services sectors.

Enforcement. In addition to potential problems with joint production ventures, globally active companies conduct many other international transactions, such as agreements on overseas distribution, patents, trademarks, and technology transfers, that also have antitrust implications. Uncertainty about the application of U.S. antitrust law to business decisions in these areas has intensified with the increasing participation of U.S. companies in overseas markets. In an effort to alleviate some of this uncertainty, the Justice Department, in November 1988, issued new enforcement guidelines for international operations.

The department's enforcement policy has a dual objective: to deter violations of U.S. antitrust laws and to ensure that confusion about enforcement policy does not prevent arrangements among companies that contribute to the international competitiveness of U.S. business.

As in the past, the revised guidelines regard as per-se illegal practices such as price-fixing or the territorial allocation of markets that clearly threaten to raise prices or restrict output. Consistent with its position on joint ventures, however, the department will not challenge a transaction if the anticompetitive risk is outweighed by procompetitive efficiency benefits.[42]

With the concept of balancing anticompetitive risk against procompetitive efficiency as a theme, the new international guidelines provide an extensive statement and illustrations of the department's general enforcement policy. They cover nearly every type of business transaction with antitrust implications, from criminal violations of the Sherman Antitrust Act to monopolization, vertical distribution restraints, and information exchanges. In the case of mergers, the guidelines take into account the effect of foreign competition in rendering moot the traditional quantitative standards of concentration applied to domestic firms.

These changes are welcome to the extent that they reduce uncertainty about the application of antitrust law. However, shifts in interpretation from one administration to the next, inspired by political rather than economic priorities, tend to diminish the effectiveness of such guidelines. In the absence of consistency, foreign customers often question the long-term reliability of U.S. suppliers.

Extraterritoriality. The extraterritorial reach of U.S. antitrust law continues to pose problems for U.S. firms. Many face real conflicts when they must ensure that their foreign operations do not violate domestic antitrust laws while conforming to the laws of the foreign country. The Justice Department acknowledges problems of this nature but reserves the option to take enforcement action against foreign conduct that has a direct, substantial, and reasonably foreseeable anticompetitive effect on U.S. commerce.[43]

Clearly, jurisdictional conflicts will not disappear as long as there are differences in the laws of different countries. However, the new guidelines stress the Justice Department's recognition that antitrust laws cannot operate in a vacuum and that enforcement will have to give way in certain circumstances—for example, when conduct is compelled by a foreign government or "when the conduct in question has a greater effect on significant foreign national interests than on U.S. interests, and deference to those foreign national interests is appropriate."[44]

On the international front, the United States is an active participant in the OECD's Committee on Competition Law and Policy. Several times a year, representatives of member countries meet under the auspices of the committee to report on changes in their respective antitrust practices and the likely international impact of these changes. Although no formal mechanism exists to harmonize the laws of member states, the effect of these regular consultations has been a gradual convergence in the way competition authorities in each country interpret their laws.

CED endorses the efforts taking place both domestically and internationally to reduce the ambiguities and jurisdictional conflicts in antitrust law and to bring enforcement into consonance with the new realities of the global economy. If successful, such efforts would effectively lower barriers to entry into new domestic and foreign markets by reducing the risks and costs associated with technology development and joint ventures.

Foreign Corrupt Practices Act

The Foreign Corrupt Practices Act (FCPA) was passed in 1977 following the disclosure of questionable payments by many U.S. firms to foreign officials during the 1960s and early 1970s. Intended to reduce corruption by U.S. companies in their international operations, the law prohibits bribery of foreign officials to win contracts and requires the use of internal accounting practices that discourage such bribery.

Because of the vagueness and ambiguity surrounding the act's intent and application, many U.S. businesses have been handicapped in competing for sales overseas. Uncertainty about the specific definition of illegal payments, confusion about appropriate accounting standards, and insufficient guidance from the Justice Department about individual situations have effectively increased the costs of conducting international business. These costs, coupled with the threat of adverse publicity stemming from even unfounded allegations of violations of the FCPA, have sometimes deterred U.S. business from pursuing legitimate commercial opportunities.

The absence of similar legislation in other major industrial countries also places American companies at a competitive disadvantage. Most nations prohibit domestic bribery, but the United States is the only country that explicitly prohibits illicit payments to foreign officials to obtain export contracts.

Recognizing its negative competitive impact, Congress attempted in the 1988 Omnibus Trade and Competitiveness Act to rectify the ambiguities in the FCPA, to clarify some of the accounting issues, and to improve the government's handling of both information requests and enforcement procedures.

To reduce definitional uncertainty, the 1988 act clarifies the distinction between a bribe to a foreign official and a "facilitating" payment to expedite the performance of routine government action. The facilitating payment is permitted as long as it is legal in the foreign country and is restricted to expediting routine actions commonly performed by the official such as processing visas, scheduling inspections, or arranging for the loading or unloading of cargo.

Payment to a foreign official or political party for the purpose of influencing a decision by the foreign government on what terms to award, retain, or renew contracts is still considered bribery under the FCPA, as is any payment to induce a foreign official to act in violation of his or her country's laws. Furthermore, both civil and criminal penalties for violating the law have been increased.

Expenses paid by a U.S. company on behalf of a foreign official for purposes such as travel or lodging are legal as long as they are directly related to the promotion, demonstration, or explanation of products or services or the execution or performance of a contract with the foreign government.

Many business executives expressed confusion about possible liability under the FCPA for the conduct of foreign agents who might be essential to doing business in a foreign country. Their concern centered on the act's "reason-to-know" standard because both direct and indirect bribes are prohibited. The Trade Act of 1988 attempts to clarify the civil and criminal liability for the payment of bribes through third parties.

The act also provides for further consultations between representatives of business and the relevant government departments to ascertain whether additional clarification of the law is needed. In any event, the Justice Department will establish a procedure to respond within thirty days to inquiries from exporters about the conformity of their plans to the law.

The accounting provisions of the FCPA were also amended. Recognizing that it is unrealistic to expect a minority owner to exert a disproportionate influence over the accounting practices of a subsidiary, the act provides that a company with less than 50 percent ownership in a foreign firm has fulfilled its responsibility if it proceeds in good faith to use its influence to cause the subsidiary to adopt accounting controls that are consistent with the FCPA.

Despite these changes, the U.S. government remains committed to the objectives of the FCPA. However, it recognizes that corruption in foreign trade and investment is, in the final analysis, an international problem. The 1988 trade act therefore stresses that multinational action is essential to eliminating corrupt practices. It requests the President to pursue negotiations within the OECD to promote cooperation in international efforts to prevent bribery.

Given the lack of specific international action on corrupt practices over the past decade, the act suggests that if international negotiations do not eliminate competitive disadvantages for U.S. businesses resulting from differences between U.S. law and the laws of other countries, the executive branch should propose appropriate actions to take in response to the situation.

We welcome the changes that have been made in the Foreign Corrupt Practices Act and fully support the vigorous pursuit of a comprehensive international agreement on corrupt practices in foreign transactions.

Product Liability

The evolution of the U.S. system of legal liability in recent years has resulted in a number of adverse consequences for the nation's economy. As a CED study explains, "the uncontrolled and uncoordinated expansion of tort liability is not only burdening U.S. business firms, service organizations, and individuals with burgeoning legal fees, court awards, and insurance costs, but also threatens to detract from our national economic well-being by raising prices, deterring the provision of certain vital goods and services, discouraging product and service innovation, and damaging U.S. international competitiveness."[45]

Differences between U.S. and foreign product liability laws can not only deter U.S. exports but also reduce the competitiveness of U.S. firms against foreigners operating in this country.

Because U.S. companies may be subject to U.S. liability rules for their products sold abroad while foreign firms can make distribution arrangements for their products sold in the United States that do not fully expose them to the provisions and penalties of U.S. law, U.S. firms tend to incur higher insurance costs per dollar of sales than do their foreign competitors.[46] One insurance company has estimated that in terms of GDP devoted to liability insurance, U.S. expenditures exceeded those of Japan, West Germany, France, Great Britain, Canada, Italy, and Australia by an average factor of four. In comparison with Japan alone, U.S. liability insurance is fifteen times higher.[47]

For industries facing high liability costs in the United States and intense competition from foreign firms in both international and domestic markets, insurance costs can make the difference between being competitive or uncompetitive. Industries subject to particularly high insurance premiums, such as pharmaceuticals, chemicals, machine tools, and general aviation, tend to be most adversely affected by this situation.

Underlying the differences in insurance premiums are several aspects of U.S. liability law that raise the costs for U.S. firms versus foreign competitors. First, the present U.S. liability system is far more advantageous to plaintiffs in both procedural and substantive law than that of any other country. Discovery rules are more generous, particularly in determining awards for noneconomic loss. The concept of punitive damages, commonly used in the United States, is completely absent in most countries.[48] Also, among major industrial countries, only the United States permits contingent fees enabling a plaintiff to bring a suit without paying legal costs up front. In the great majority of countries, liability suits are decided by judges, not juries. As a result of these differences, it is easier to sue and receive higher awards and settlements in the United States. Taken together, these factors produce a more expensive liability system and therefore higher costs to firms requiring insurance to protect themselves.

Furthermore, although in principle foreign manufacturers selling in U.S. markets are subject to the same liabilities as domestic firms, in practice they have significant procedural advantages. For example, the less generous discovery rules in a foreign firm's home country may apply even to litigation in the United States, at least with respect to the company's records outside this country.[49] Similarly, the costs of collecting a judgment against a foreign firm are often higher. Many foreign firms operate in the United States through independent export agents or wholly owned subsidiaries, whose assets may be insufficient for a plaintiff to recover large damages. As a consequence, foreign firms face lower expected costs of being sued in the United States than their U.S. competitors do.

The expensive product liability system in which U.S. firms must function also results in indirect costs that may place them at a disadvantage when competing abroad. For example, in an effort to reduce the possibility of being sued, U.S. firms may incur greater production costs than their foreign counterparts whose products reflect less stringent liability regimes and a less litigious environment in their home countries.[50] If the foreign consumer does not perceive added value in the final product, the competitiveness of a U.S. manufacturer/exporter may be undermined in foreign markets.[51]

For the United States to maintain a competitive position in international markets, serious consideration should be given to the international context of the liability system's operation. To produce more equitable competition internationally while still affording consumers in each country the protection to which they are accustomed, we recommend the following changes in the liability system based on the principle of national treatment in international trade:

- Foreign litigants desiring to sue U.S. producers for injuries incurred outside the United States should bring suit in the country where the injury occurred, which will usually be their own country. To forestall bringing such cases into U.S. courts, all U.S. courts should deny access to such foreign litigants, as most federal courts already do. Our aim here is to achieve a more level playing field between foreign-based and domestic-based sellers of products.

- Foreign sellers of products in the United States should be subject to financial responsibility requirements as stringent as those applied to U.S. firms. This will assure U.S. consumers the same tort rights against foreign-based suppliers as against domestic firms.[52]

Over the longer term, it would be desirable for major countries to harmonize their product liability laws, which are so vastly different today.

Environmental Regulation

There are significant differences among countries in expenditures on pollution control. According to a 1985 OECD study, expenditures on pollution control as a percentage of GDP were higher in the United States than in any other OECD country for which data were available.[53] It is likely that even greater differences exist between the industrialized and less developed countries, and these discrepancies inevitably contribute to differences in production costs. Although the effect on U.S. international competitiveness of our relatively high environmental standards is minor for most industries, it is substantial in some sectors, such as nonferrous metals.

In the United States, the benefits from environmental regulations in terms of a safer and healthier quality of life are widely recognized. However, some less developed countries have chosen to become pollution havens, thereby sacrificing their environment for economic reasons. Therefore, they could be seen as exporting environmental quality along with their lower-priced goods. At some point, however, these countries, too, will need to raise their environmental standards and expenditures to be more consistent with those of developed countries, both for their own sake and for the world's.

One can ask whether pollution control should be a necessary aspect of modern production for all nations. Condemnation of polluters seems appropriate for types of pollution that damage the environment beyond the borders of the offending nation and where the benefits of pollution reduction would be correspondingly dispersed.

Given the effect on production costs of environmental regulations, the question arises whether the concept of unfair trade practices should include the failure of a country to maintain environmental standards or the subsidization by a government of private-sector pollution-abatement costs. If so, should the equivalent of antidumping or countervailing duties be imposed on imports from such a country?

This issue was addressed by the OECD in 1972, when it adopted a set of principles to guide the industrial countries in their trade policy regarding environmental measures. In essence, the principles recognize the legitimacy of differences in national environmental standards that reflect such factors as differences in income levels and the assimilative capacity of the environment. A country's exports should therefore not be penalized through trade restrictions for its failure to maintain the same environmental standards as other countries. However, when pollution-abatement costs are incurred in the private sector, they should be borne there rather than by the government so that market prices will more accurately reflect the social costs of production. To the extent that this *polluter-pays* principle is followed, border tax adjustments to offset differences in environmental costs are unjustified.

These principles have served as guidelines for the industrial countries, but many developing countries have not subscribed to them. Nor have the nations of the Third World developed any guidelines of their own. With the rapid growth of developing-country trade in an integrated global economy, we believe Third World nations should be encouraged to develop a set of guidelines in the environmental field that minimize distortions in international trade.

Increasing attention is being directed to potentially serious environmental problems that transcend national boundaries, such as greenhouse warming and ozone depletion. We support a multilateral approach as the only effective way of addressing these problems.

Tax Legislation

U.S. tax laws can exert a powerful influence, either positive or negative, on the international competitive position of U.S. goods and services in the global marketplace. We have therefore consistently held that U.S. tax policy as applied to the foreign operations of U.S. companies should be sensitive to avoiding unreasonable and detrimental burdens on international trade and investment, particularly when our major trading partners do not impose comparable burdens on their own multinational firms.[54]

The 1986 tax legislation is a case in point. Although several provisions in the law relate explicitly to the international operations of U.S. companies, it is widely acknowledged that these provisions were developed with little attention to their potentially adverse impact on the international competitiveness of U.S. companies. The following provisions are of particular concern:

- New separate provisions eliminating low-taxed passive income and a number of other separate categories of income from the averaging mechanism in computing the overall foreign tax credit. The result is a considerable loss of flexibility for some multinationals.

• Changes in the method for allocating interest, research and development, and other expenses to offset foreign income, resulting in losses of deductions that will both increase costs for international companies and militate against research and development investment in this country.

• The introduction of the concept of a superroyalty that requires multinationals to include in their U.S. taxable income amounts that are commensurate with the income attributable to intangible properties originated in the United States.

• Foreign tax credit limitations on dividends of joint ventures or of subsidiaries in which U.S. corporations own a minority interest.

To avoid potential damage to the U.S. competitive position in world markets, we recommend an early review of the 1986 revisions in the tax treatment of foreign operations of U.S. firms that takes the U.S. competitive position into careful account and such modifications in the provisions as may be appropriate in light of this review.

Notes

1. The Gephardt amendment was aimed at countries with "excessive" trade surpluses with the United States and a "pattern of unfair trade practices." If this situation were not remedied by negotiation, the President would have been required to adopt measures to reduce the country's bilateral surplus by 10 percent each year.

2. Text of remarks by the President of the United States to the U.S. Chamber of Commerce Foundation's Reagan Legacy Conference (The White House, Office of the Press Secretary, Washington, D.C., November 17, 1988).

3. "When the dollar fell relative to the yen after 1985, many Japanese firms responded by cutting the yen prices of their exports in order to hold down the dollar prices of their products in U.S. markets. At the same time, they kept the prices of their goods sold inside Japan relatively constant. The result, according to NBER Research Associate Richard Marston, has been that the yen prices of Japanese exports have fallen sharply relative to the prices of the same goods sold in Japan. Marston concludes that this shows that the Japanese markets may be closed not only to foreign products but even to the re-import of Japanese products." National Bureau of Economic Research, "Japanese Pricing at Home and Abroad," *The NBER Digest* (May 1989), p. 3.

4. There are at least two important exceptions to the rule that the administration of the antidumping laws is insulated from political considerations. One is when the Commerce Department initiates an antidumping proceeding, as it did in the steel and semiconductor cases. Another is when Commerce suspends

an investigation when the alleged foreign dumpers agree to certain undertakings. Political considerations weigh heavily in these decisions.

5. Data on escape-clause cases are from the International Trade Commission. For countervailing-duty and antidumping cases, data are from J. Michael Finger and Andrzei Olechowski, eds., *The Uruguay Round: A Handbook on the Multilateral Trade Negotiations* (Washington, D.C.: The World Bank, 1987), Appendix Tables 8.1 and 8.3. Cases are classified as affirmative in these tables if there was a "definitive duty" or "price undertaking" or "other action."

6. Although antidumping and countervailing-duty cases still greatly outnumber escape-clause cases, they declined noticeably in the most recent twelve-month period compared with the average number of cases in the previous three years. *Journal of Commerce,* August 29, 1989.

7. John H. Barton and Bart S. Fisher, *International Trade and Investment* (Boston: Little Brown and Company, 1986), pp. 299–300.

8. Another route to back-door protection in the antidumping law has been through the adoption of technical amendments and regulatory practices which determine the adjustments that are made to prices in the home and export markets before they are compared to determine whether dumping exists. Some of these adjustments have no rational basis and inflate dumping margins.

9. Finger and Olechowski, *The Uruguay Round,* pp. 157 and 259.

10. *OECD National Accounts,* various issues, as reproduced in International Monetary Fund, *Issues and Developments in International Trade Policy,* Occasional Paper 63 (Paris, December 1988), Appendix Table 11.

11. GATT, Article XVI.4, applying to developed countries that signed the 1960 declaration giving effect to this provision.

12. Based on a conversation with Joseph Pechman of the Brookings Institution, who edited *World Tax Reform: A Progress Report* (Washington, D.C.: Brookings Institution, 1988).

The feasibility of extending border adjustments to direct taxes is also questionable. The large firms that account for a substantial proportion of U.S. foreign trade produce hundreds of different products. For the purpose of rebates, how would a company's income tax payments be allocated among its multiple products? What rate of tax would be imposed on imports of products that the United States does not produce at all, such as subcompact automobiles, which may nevertheless be competitive at the margin with compact domestic cars. And suppose that for a given product, some domestic producers earn a profit but others suffer losses. What would be the basis for the border tax adjustments?

A related issue is whether the United States, as part of its program to reduce the budgetary deficit, should adopt a consumption tax that could be imposed on imports and rebated on exports. However, this proposal raises a number of basic issues of fiscal policy that transcend the adjustability of the tax at the border.

13. C. Fred Bergsten, *America in the World Economy: A Strategy for the 1990s* (Washington, D.C.: Institute for International Economics, November 1988), pp. 133–134.

14. Gary Hufbauer and Joanna Erb, *Subsidies in International Trade* (Washington, D.C.: Institute for International Economics, 1984), p. 117.

15. GATT Code on Subsidies and Countervailing Duties, Article X.

16. During 1984–1986, the costs of agricultural supports to consumers and taxpayers in the major industrial countries averaged about $185 billion annually. *IMF Survey,* 17, no. 23 (December 12, 1988), p. 389.

17. Thomas R. Howell et al., *Steel and the State: Government Intervention and Steel's Structural Crisis* (Boulder: Westview Press, 1988).

18. Investigations by the U.S. Commerce Department and the ITC revealed extremely high margins of subsidization and dumping by European suppliers. The margin of subsidization on most imports from British Steel was 20.33 percent; on imports from France's Sacilor and Usinor, margins ranged from 11.3 to 21.42 percent; and the margins on many other producers were substantial, including Italsider (14.56 percent) and Cockerill Sambre (13.44 percent). Many of the heavily subsidized firms were also found to be dumping by substantial margins. West German (Thyssen) margins of dumping ranged as high as 19.17 percent. See Howell et al., *Steel and the State,* p. 523.

19. For a fuller discussion of the factors underlying the improvement of the U.S. steel industry's competitiveness, see U.S. General Accounting Office, *International Trade: The Health of the U.S. Steel Industry* (Washington, D.C., July 1989).

20. United States International Trade Commission, *The Effects of the Steel Voluntary Restraint Agreements on U.S. Steel-Consuming Industries* (Washington, D.C., May 1989), p. vii.

21. According to the ITC, the VRAs caused increases in the prices of imported steel in the United States that averaged 1.7 percent in 1985, 4.3 percent in 1986, 4.2 percent in 1987, and 0.5 percent in 1988. The VRAs caused increases in prices of domestically produced steel that averaged 0.2 percent in 1985, 0.5 percent in 1986 and 1987, and 0.1 percent in 1988. The weighted-average increases in the prices of imported and domestic steel caused by VRAs were 0.6 percent in 1985, 1.6 percent in 1986, 1.4 percent in 1987, and 0.2 percent in 1988. ITC, *The Effects of Steel Voluntary Restraint Agreements on U.S. Steel-Consuming Industries,* p. vii.

22. Howell et al., *Steel and the State,* p. 541.

23. "American Steel: Did You Say De-Industrializing?" *The Economist,* December 17, 1988, p. 75.

24. Office of the U.S. Trade Representative, *1989 National Trade Estimate Report on Foreign Trade Barriers* (Washington, D.C., 1989). The 1989 report delineates barriers in thirty-four nations and two trading blocs.

25. Insurance is a state monopoly in India. Liberalization of India's insurance market would create significant opportunities for U.S. insurance companies that are competitive worldwide.

26. Office of the U.S. Trade Representative, *The President's Trade Policy: An Update* (Washington, D.C., June 15, 1988).

27. Makota Kuroda, "We've Had Enough of John Wayne," *The International Economy* (November-December 1988), p. 67.

28. Sections 1371 to 1382 of the Trade Act address these issues, and Part 4 of the act may be referred to as the "Telecommunications Trade Act of 1988."

29. European Community, *1988 Report on U.S. Trade Barriers* (Brussels, December 1987).

30. Adam Smith, *Wealth of Nations* (New York: Random House, The Modern Library, 1985), pp. 237–238.

31. In December 1988, the United States threatened retaliation to stop the EC from applying to U.S. exports its ban on meat from animals treated with growth hormones. Although the ban was labeled a health measure applying to all meat for human consumption, whether domestically produced or imported, the United States contended that it had no scientific basis. To Europeans, the case was comparable to the American ban on imports of cheese made from unpasteurized milk, a product widely consumed in Europe. Because the Europeans had accepted the American ban without threatening retaliation, they saw no reason why the United States should not accommodate to the European action. The Community warned that if the United States carried out its threat to retaliate, they would counterretaliate, and Washington had counterwarned that it would counter the counterretaliation. Although the issue has been resolved for the present, the friction threatened to damage the overall $150 billion-a-year trade relationship between the United States and the European Community.

32. Carla A. Hills, United States Trade Representative, in a letter to the editor of *The Economist,* May 20, 1989, p. 4.

33. Gary Clyde Hufbauer, "Background Paper," in Twentieth Century Fund, *The Free Trade Debate* (New York: Priority Press Publications, 1989), p. 60 and Table 2.4 on p. 168.

34. "Background Paper" by Hufbauer in *The Free Trade Debate* refers only to barriers imposed by industrial countries. It is true that import restrictions are higher in the developing countries than in the United States, but there is no evidence that they have increased in recent years nor that these countries systematically discriminate against the United States.

35. This method can even lead to a perverse result: The more restrictive the barrier on a particular product, the less the imports of that product, and therefore the *lower* the proportion of trade subject to restriction.

36. *Basic Framework of GATT Provisions on Intellectual Property: Statement of Views of the European, Japanese, and United States Business Communities* (June 1988).

37. Office of the U.S. Trade Representative, *Fact Sheet on "Special 301" on Intellectual Property* (Washington, D.C., May 25, 1989).

38. National Academy of Sciences, *Balancing the National Interest: National Security Export Controls and Global Economic Competition* (Washington, D.C.: National Academy Press, 1987).

39. Gary Clyde Hufbauer and Jeffrey J. Schott, *Economic Sanctions in Support of Foreign Policy Goals* (Washington, D.C.: Institute for International Economics, October 1983).

40. *Overview and Compilation of U.S. Trade Statutes* (1989 edition), Committee on Ways and Means, U.S. House of Representatives, Washington, D.C., pp. 121–122.

41. Ibid., p. 122.

42. Charles F. Rule, Assistant Attorney General, Antitrust Division, U.S. Department of Justice, "The Justice Department's Antitrust Enforcement Guidelines for International Operations—A Competition Policy for the 1990s" (Remarks before the International Trade Section and Antitrust Committee of the District of Columbia Bar, Washington, D.C., November 29, 1988).

43. Rule, "The Justice Department's Antitrust Guidelines for International Operations," p. 15.

44. Ibid., p. 18.

45. Committee for Economic Development, *Who Should Be Liable? A Guide to Policy for Dealing with Risk* (1989), p. x.

46. CED, *Who Should Be Liable?* p. 94–96: Precise country-to-country comparisons of insurance costs are extremely difficult because of differences in policy limits and policy terms between countries.

47. Ibid., p. 96, citing letter dated March 7, 1988, from George Zacharokow, President, Marine and International Group, Continental Insurance to J. H. Bretherick of Continental Insurance, forwarded to Charles F. Barber. These expenditures excluded auto liability insurance, for which the United States also led.

48. Ibid., p. 94, which cites Douglas J. Besharov: "Liability for Foreign Torts: Whose Law Should Apply?" (Paper prepared for Round Table Conference on the Impact of U.S. Product Liability Laws on U.S. Export Trade and International Competitiveness, The Fletcher School of Law and Diplomacy, Tufts University, Boston, October 4–6, 1987), p. 3.

49. CED, *Who Should Be Liable?* p. 95, which notes that in many countries outside the United States, disclosure of corporate records is a crime. Besharov, "Liability for Foreign Torts," p. 11.

50. In general, U.S. firms selling in the United States and foreign markets tend to have uniform policies worldwide, so that liability-induced improvements are executed even in places where the liability may not apply. Because of economies of scale, it is not cost-effective for them to have different product lines or different policies regarding risk, one for domestic and one for foreign markets. For some large firms, however, this is feasible. See CED, *Who Should Be Liable?* p. 96.

51. It can be argued that the reverse is also true: that foreign producers selling products in the United States that are designed primarily for a less safety-conscious foreign market are at a disadvantage relative to U.S. producers. Like any barrier to imports, this could benefit domestic producers but reduce product choice for domestic consumers. In practice, foreign firms are still considered to benefit overall, for the disadvantage of selling in a safety-conscious environment is often outweighed by the lower probability of suit against foreign firms.

52. CED, *Who Should Be Liable?* p. 13.

53. Organization for Economic Cooperation and Development, *Environment and Economics: Results of the International Conference on Environment and Economics, 18–21 June 1984* (Paris, 1985), p. 50.

54. Recent CED statements on tax policy are contained in *Tax Reform for a Productive Economy* (1985) and *Toll of the Twin Deficits* (1987).

4

Multilateral Versus
Alternative Approaches

For three and a half decades after World War II, the United States pursued a trade policy firmly grounded in the principles of multilateralism and nondiscrimination.[1] Exceptions were rare. Indeed, in the early postwar years, this country was the main advocate of arrangements based on these principles and the main opponent of discriminatory schemes. In the past decade, however, U.S. exceptions have grown in number and importance.

For the most part, exceptions to the tradition of multilateralism and nondiscrimination have taken the form of bilateral arrangements to *restrict* foreign access to the U.S. market for certain products, such as steel. In this chapter, we focus primarily on the exceptions whose objective has been to *liberalize* trade. The most important has been the comprehensive free trade agreement negotiated with Canada, this country's largest single trading partner. The growing inclination of U.S. policy makers to pursue trade-liberalizing arrangements outside the traditional framework of multilateralism has been mainly a reaction to their growing frustration.

One frustration is grounded in the perception that multilateral arrangements, which have established both the rules of the game and procedures for resolving disputes, have failed to create trading opportunities for American exporters equivalent to the opportunities foreign exporters enjoy in the U.S. market. Many believe that other countries fail to abide by the negotiated rules and that procedures to resolve disputes are slow and produce unsatisfactory results. As a consequence, the notion that the United States should seek reciprocal conditions of market access in specific sectors as a primary objective of its trade policy has attracted support as U.S. primacy in the world economy has eroded and as U.S. trade deficits have ballooned to unprecedented levels. Moreover, the notion that the United States has the right, our inter-

national obligations notwithstanding, to take retaliatory action against
countries that refuse to grant us unilateral concessions to achieve reciprocal conditions of market access has also gained support.

A second frustration (the one most keenly felt by the Reagan administration) is that multilateral arrangements have not evolved to
include new areas of trade that are of keen interest to the United States.
In the early 1980s, the United States attempted to cajole its trading
partners to renew the process of multilateral negotiations with the
objective of reaching agreements on such matters as trade in services,
trade-related investment measures, and the protection of intellectual
property rights, but its efforts met with little success. Now, those
negotiations are finally under way, but they were too long in coming
and their outcome is still in doubt.

A third frustration arises from the perception that the economies of
some other major countries do not operate in conformity with the
implicit assumptions upon which the multilateral rules are based. Two
economies may be market-driven and yet behave in significantly different ways because their cultures and histories produce different un-
derstandings of the same concepts (such as openness and fairness) and
different ways of organizing and carrying out similar economic functions. The application of universal rules in these circumstances places
the United States at a disadvantage in the eyes of some observers. They
advocate rules tailored to the particular circumstances of bilateral
trading relationships. Some go so far as advocating the negotiation of
specific trade outcomes, in terms of volume or market share, on a
bilateral basis, thus mandating *results* rather than relying on opportunities to trade based on universal rules and open competition.

In sum, the tendency toward exceptions has been motivated by a
spreading conviction that the single-minded pursuit of multilateralism
no longer adequately serves U.S. interests.

The persistence of these frustrations, the success of negotiations with
Canada to create a landmark free trade agreement, and the progress of
the European Community toward constructing a truly single market—
embodied in the concept of 1992—prompt compelling questions. Should
the United States pursue other discriminatory trade arrangements?
Should the pursuit of such arrangements play a more central role in
U.S. trade policy? Should such arrangements remain the exception in
U.S. policy, or should they become the rule? What are the implications,
both for the United States and for the world trading system, of such a
policy change? Where do U.S. interests lie?

The analysis which follows leads us to the conclusion that U.S.
interests will best be served by preserving multilateralism as the guiding
principle of U.S. trade policy. We also recognize that special circum-

stances may arise, as in the Canadian case, in which exceptions to that principle are warranted. At present, we see only very limited opportunities to advance U.S. interests through such arrangements. The exploration of a special trade (and quite possibly broader economic) arrangement with Mexico is the sole exception we see on the horizon. Fundamentally, we are convinced that discriminatory arrangements should remain exceptions to the general rule of multilateralism governing U.S. policy.

The principle of multilateralism is embodied in GATT. GATT is an agreement establishing rules for world trade, a mechanism through which trade disputes can be resolved, and the instrument through which the liberalization of world trade has been negotiated over the past forty years. However, GATT has serious shortcomings, both as a rule book and as a resolver of disputes. For many frustrated American traders it has come to symbolize the reasons why the principle of multilateralism may no longer be an appropriate guide to pursuing U.S. interests.

GATT is, of course, a creature of its members. Its most serious problem has been a lack of will to make it work effectively. The jury is still out on the question of whether the will exists to improve GATT to better serve world trade and U.S. interests. The jury is now assembled for the Uruguay Round of multilateral trade negotiations, trying to meet the challenges of making GATT more effective. The success of the Uruguay Round is of the greatest importance to the United States. This country's interests require that its energies and resources be devoted to achieving success there and not diluted by the pursuit of alternative trade arrangements.

The Tradition of Multilateralism and Nondiscrimination

Origins and Achievements

Santayana warned that those who cannot remember the past are condemned to repeat it. That may be a cliché now, but it is nevertheless worth heeding. When the authors of GATT adopted the unconditional Most-Favored-Nation (MFN) provision,[2] which lies at the agreement's heart and which embodies the principles of multilateralism and nondiscrimination, they were applying lessons learned from harsh experience. They understood that discriminatory trading arrangements had been an important cause of the international tensions leading to World War II.

American trade policy in the late 1930s aimed to negotiate a network of reciprocal, bilateral agreements to lower tariffs and to end discrimination against U.S. exports. Most of the rest of the world was headed

in quite a different direction, however. The dominant trend in commercial policy was the forging of agreements that increased discrimination and raised trade restrictions. These agreements were motivated
by highly nationalistic economic policies and contributed to prolonging
the worst depression in modern times.

Even before the United States entered World War II, American
business and political leaders saw spheres of economic influence evolv-
ing—Europe controlled by Germany, Africa dominated by Europe, Asia
dominated by Japan, and the United States confined to influence in
North and South America—that were fundamentally at odds with
America's interests. When the opportunity came after the war to create
a new world economic order, the architects of the GATT set out quite
deliberately to fashion an antidote to what had gone before. Their
antidote was multilateralism and nondiscrimination, which thereafter
became the foundation for both U.S. trade policy and global trade
arrangements.

In the decades following the war, trade flourished, and economic
growth advanced at an unprecedented pace. The movement toward
multilateralism and away from preferential arrangements and the reduction of trade barriers on a nondiscriminatory basis may not have
been a sufficient condition for this expansion of trade and growth to
occur, but it was certainly a necessary condition. The experience gives
strong support to the proposition that freer trade on a nondiscriminatory
basis promotes growth and increases welfare, one of the most robust
conclusions to emerge from the study of economics.

The most obvious direct achievement of the successive rounds of
multilateral trade negotiations has been the reduction of tariffs. It is a
result we take for granted today, but it has nonetheless been a significant
achievement. With some notable exceptions,[3] tariffs no longer constitute
a significant barrier to trade among the industrial countries.

The multilateral, nondiscriminatory framework for negotiations has
also proved to be an efficient way to deal with a number of countries
simultaneously. Generalizing the results of trade liberalization to all
GATT members undoubtedly produced more liberalization and therefore more trade expansion quicker than could otherwise have occurred.
No doubt the growth of trade was also facilitated by the greater efficiency
with which national customs officials could clear imported goods for
distribution without the concern for their origin that would be required
under a discriminatory system.

The acceptance of multilateralism and nondiscrimination also made
possible full participation in the world economy by a growing number
of nations. Expanding participation in the system was a positive force
for growth and for increasing world welfare.

Finally, the multilateral, nondiscriminatory approach achieved the original goal of its architects: It helped to combat the centrifugal forces in the world economy that had been so politically destabilizing before World War II.

Challenges

To a considerable extent, the GATT-based system of trade has been a victim of its own success. The growing number of participating countries and the progressive reduction of tariffs created new problems with which nations have so far coped with only limited success. These problems have exposed shortcomings in the multilateral, nondiscriminatory system that pose challenges to the system's effective operation and therefore to its durability.

Negotiation Dynamics. Multilateral trade liberalization is made difficult and slow by two problems at the root of much of the U.S. frustration that is propelling an interest in alternative trade arrangements: the free rider and the convoy.[4]

There is a natural incentive for negotiators operating in a multilateral arena to withhold concessions in the hope that they can benefit from the generalization of others' concessions without making their own. The only way to avoid such free riders—a role that the United States, as the system's leader, can rarely if ever play—is for everyone to make concessions at the same time. This means that the pace of progress in negotiations is determined by the least willing major participant, just as the speed of a convoy is dictated by the speed of its slowest ship.

The free-rider and convoy problems have been exacerbated by three phenomena associated with the success of the postwar trading system. The first is simply the dramatic growth in the number of relevant participants. The *multi* in multilateral implies a much larger number of countries today than it did in 1948. As the number of countries participating in GATT negotiations has grown from twenty-three to ninety-six, and as some of the previously minor participants in the trading system have developed into major players, the task of forging an international consensus has become more difficult. Reflecting this, the seven successive rounds of multilateral trade negotiations have taken longer and longer to complete.

A related problem is the participation of countries at dramatically different stages of economic development. Some developing countries have been among the most reluctant to expand the scope of multilateral rules. They fear that the constraints on their behavior new rules would impose would handicap their efforts to catch up with the industrial nations. These countries have been the laggards in the convoy moving

toward agreements on trade in services, trade-related investment measures, and protection of intellectual property rights.

The second phenomenon has been the reluctance of all countries to
bear the adjustment costs of participating in a dynamic international
economy. As tariffs have declined and trade has expanded, the adjustment costs—that is, the economic dislocation countries must endure as
the price of progress—have grown larger. Countries seek to avoid or
at least minimize these costs and have become creative in substituting
nontariff barriers for tariffs. As the pace and cost of adjustment have
risen, so too has the difficulty of negotiating multilateral rules to impose
discipline on nontariff barriers.

The third phenomenon has been the *relative* decline of the power of
the United States. As the most basic objectives of postwar U.S. foreign
economic policy were realized—economic recovery in Western Europe
and Japan and rising standards of living in the world generally—the
United States ironically found itself less and less able to exert decisive
influence in directing the process of rule making and the pace of
liberalization.

By 1982, the convoy problem had worsened to the point that it
paralyzed the ability of countries to pursue multilateral liberalization.
That year, despite strong entreaties from the United States and some
other countries, a GATT ministerial meeting failed to reach agreement
on an agenda for a new round of multilateral trade negotiations. To
the extent that the turn in U.S. trade policy away from the singular
pursuit of trade agreements based on multilateralism and nondiscrimination had a proximate cause, the 1982 GATT ministerial meeting
was that cause. More than any other single event, it prompted the
search for alternatives to multilateral liberalization under the GATT.

The timing of the 1982 meeting was significant. It occurred in the
midst of a severe U.S. recession, when, largely as a consequence of
flawed macroeconomic policies, the U.S. trade account was turning
sharply negative and the dollar's value was moving sharply upward.
The tradable goods sector of the U.S. economy came under severe
pressure that was clearly reflected in rising protectionist sentiment
among U.S. industry and labor and in Congress. Suggestions by U.S.
officials in the wake of the GATT ministerial that the United States
was prepared to explore alternative ways to achieve its trade-liberalizing
objectives fell on fertile ground. Two U.S. trading partners with major
stakes in access to the U.S. market, first Israel and then Canada,
responded to this combination of danger and opportunity by initiating
the negotiation of free trade agreements with the United States.

Adversity in Diversity. The postwar trading system was designed by
American and British architects who drafted rules grounded in implicit

assumptions that reflected their own experience with the role of gov-ernment in the economy, with the ownership and structure of industry, with rules governing competition, and with how trade is conducted. At the time, with a preponderance of European and North American participants and with tariffs the main obstacle to trade, there was little reason to question the validity of those assumptions. But forty years later, there is.

The substantial elimination of tariffs as obstacles to trade has made apparent the fact that a much broader variety of national policies, practices, and customs influences trade flows. These factors are inherent in the ways different societies organize themselves to carry on economic activity. The problem has been made much more complex by the growing importance in the trading system of countries whose economies flow from cultural traditions and histories radically different from those of the system's original European and North American members. The implications of this fact for the design and implementation of universal rules governing world trade are troublesome.

Problems of Scope. The problems inherent in multilateral negotiating dynamics in a world of diverse economic systems are magnified when countries try to cope with commercial policy problems much more complex than reducing tariffs on merchandise trade. The growing so-phistication and the heightened integration of the world economy, made possible by the postwar system of multilateral and nondiscriminatory trade, have spawned issues related to trade and investment, trade in services, and the protection of intellectual property rights. Addressing these issues would have presented major challenges to the original participants in the system, even with their limited numbers and more homogeneous economic systems; the challenge to negotiators today is staggering.

The Tradition of Exceptions

Exceptions

Although multilateralism and nondiscrimination have guided most trade arrangements over the past forty years, there have been notable exceptions. The architects of the postwar system acknowledged that potential benefits lay in arrangements outside the most-favored-nation mainstream (if certain conditions were met) and made explicit provision in GATT for some of them. Additional arrangements evolved as ad hoc solutions to problems that arose over the years. The exceptions are large enough in number and importance to constitute a tradition of their own. The United States has had experience with these arrangements as both an insider and an outsider. This experience must be assessed in pondering the future course of U.S. policy.

The common denominator of this tradition of exceptions is that all the arrangements have been discriminatory in nature. But they have been of two fundamentally different characters: trade-liberalizing and trade-restricting. In the trade-liberalizing category belong free trade agreements and customs unions that conform to GATT requirements, as well as plurilateral agreements governing discreet areas of trade such as the codes of conduct negotiated in the Tokyo Round of multilateral trade negotiations. In the trade-restricting category belong sectoral arrangements such as those that now apply to trade in textiles and apparel, steel, and motor vehicles and that threaten to be applied to a wider range of products.

Free Trade Areas. In a free trade area (FTA), countries agree to eliminate barriers on all or substantially all the trade among the members. However, each country independently maintains its own restrictions relative to countries outside the group. Because successive rounds of multilateral negotiations have reduced tariffs to relatively low levels, FTAs have evolved to address not only remaining tariffs but also quantitative restrictions and other nontariff barriers and to impose discipline in areas of trade and international investment where no multilateral rules exist. Examples are the European Free Trade Area (EFTA)[5] and the U.S.-Canada Free Trade Agreement.

In recent years, proposals have been advanced to carry the FTA concept even further, moving beyond commercial policy to include macroeconomic policy coordination and cooperation in managing exchange rates and solving other economic problems of mutual interest (such as LDC debt). No operating examples of such comprehensive economic agreements exist.

Customs Unions. A customs union is an FTA in which the member countries maintain a common external tariff toward outside countries and pursue a common commercial policy toward nonmembers. The European Community is the world's only flourishing customs union. (For the balance of this statement, we will use Free Trade Areas or FTAs to include customs unions.)

Conditional MFN Agreements. Countries have negotiated agreements governing certain functional areas of trade (as opposed to product-focused undertakings) that extend the benefits of the agreement *only* to those countries joining the agreement and thereby assuming its obligations. Sometimes called *plurilateral agreements,* they may hold participation open to *any* country willing to assume the agreements' obligations. Examples are the several codes—for example, on technical barriers to trade and on government procurement—negotiated during the Tokyo Round.

Sectoral Trade Agreements. Countries have negotiated a host of arrangements governing trade in selected products. In theory, such agreements can liberalize trade. For example, the 1965 U.S.-Canada Automotive Products Trade Agreement rationalized North American automotive production and, subject to certain significant limitations, liberalized bilateral trade in motor vehicles and original equipment components between Canada and the United States.

More often, however, sectoral agreements restrict or manage trade. The examples of this phenomenon have grown in number and importance in recent years. Among the most notable are the Multifiber Arrangement (actually a multilateral umbrella for the negotiation of bilateral agreements, which originated in the 1960s) governing trade in textiles and apparel, the network of so-called voluntary restraints that limit Japanese automobile exports to the United States, Canada, the European Community (as well as to certain EC member countries separately), and the bilateral arrangements that restrict U.S. steel imports. A new hybrid phenomenon is agreements that manage trade in specified products in the name of enforcing multilateral rules such as those proscribing dumping and export subsidies. The agreements restricting U.S. steel imports have been justified in part on these grounds, but the accord between the United States and Japan managing trade in semiconductors is the prototype.

Theoretical and Legal Foundations for Exceptions

Theory. A substantial body of economic theory and research addresses the implications of FTAs and customs unions, but much of it is based on the assumption that tariffs constitute the only barrier to trade. Consequently, theory and research are imprecise guides at best to appropriate U.S. policy. Nonetheless, their observations can inform our thinking about the proper course of U.S. policy.

The main point that emerges from classical theory is that even *free trade* arrangements which depart from multilateral, nondiscriminatory principles do not necessarily improve international efficiency and raise real incomes. Discriminatory free trade arrangements may be *trade-creating*—when the reduction of barriers leads a member country to import from another member what it previously produced itself—and therefore improve efficiency and raise incomes. But because such arrangements are inherently discriminatory, they may also be *trade-diverting*—when a member country merely shifts the source of its imports from a traditional foreign supplier to its new FTA partner—

and merely rearrange trade flows in a way that reduces overall efficiency and incomes. FTAs typically have both trade-creating and trade-diverting effects, and classical theory instructs us to evaluate any FTA on the basis of which effect dominates.

An important complication needs to be added to this simple picture. FTAs can have significant *dynamic* effects. In the classical analysis, countries outside an FTA cannot benefit from it in the short run because the only effects they experience are trade diversion. Over time, however, such countries can benefit.

The enlargement of a market through the negotiation of an FTA creates opportunities to achieve efficiencies leading to more rapid growth. Efficiencies are created by the realization of economies of scale that did not exist before, as well as by more vigorous competition that stimulates investment and facilitates technological progress. To the extent that these potential consequences are realized, FTAs will have dynamic, growth-creating effects that will stimulate trade with, and therefore benefit, countries outside the FTA as well as other members.

Law. The GATT recognizes the potential gains to world trade from FTAs and therefore sanctions their negotiation. To help ensure that trade creation dominates trade diversion, GATT (in Article XXIV) insists that FTAs meet three main conditions: (1) that restrictions be removed on "substantially all of the trade" between the parties to an agreement, (2) that this scope of coverage must be achieved within a reasonable amount of time pursuant to a specific plan, and (3) that barriers to countries outside the agreement may not be raised as a result of any FTA.

The logic behind these provisions is straightforward. Partial agreements are much more likely than comprehensive agreements to result in trade diversion. Permitting countries to pick and choose among products that will be covered by an FTA is likely to lead merely to replacing former foreign suppliers with FTA partners. Substituting one foreign supplier for another is not likely to cause substantial dislocation (i.e., economic pain) in either country. Given the freedom to pick and choose among products to be included within an FTA, negotiators facing the prospect of defending their actions to adversely affected special interests are more likely to choose the products that will result in trade diversion rather than trade creation.

Agreements that *raise* barriers to third-country trade can only be motivated by a desire to divert trade to FTA partners with whom barriers are being eliminated. If the margin of preference for an FTA partner over a third-country supplier must be increased beyond the preference resulting solely from the elimination of the barriers to trade between FTA partners, the resulting economic distortion must presumably be greater.

Two qualifications to these conclusions must be noted: The replacement of tariffs with nontariff measures, particularly quantitative restraints, raises questions about the validity of the GATT's "substantially all" test as a guide to judging the desirability of an FTA. Sectoral negotiations to relax quantitative restraints on trade with other FTA members should not lead to trade diversion unless restraints on trade with third countries are tightened at the same time. If third-country quantitative restraints are not tightened, an argument can be made that a partial FTA agreement will promote efficiency at no cost to outside suppliers.

Also, a partial agreement can be a stepping-stone to a comprehensive agreement. This was the expectation and the result of the European Coal and Steel Community. That agreement was conceived as a step toward a more general economic and political union, and it led in a short time to the formation of the European Community. It is also possible to think of the 1965 U.S.-Canada Automotive Products Trade Agreement as a step toward the 1988 U.S.-Canada Free Trade Agreement, but only as an accident of history. The automotive agreement was the solution to a contentious trade dispute triggered by a Canadian subsidy and the threatened imposition of a U.S. countervailing duty. Nevertheless, the generally successful experience of the two countries under the automotive pact was a confidence builder and a stimulant to the consideration of a broader agreement.

U.S. Experience with Exceptions: An Insider's View

The United States is currently a participant in two FTAs, a regional trade preference scheme, numerous bilateral sectoral trade schemes, and several plurilateral conditional MFN agreements. This patchwork quilt of arrangements is the result of years of ad hoc responses to special problems and opportunities, not the product of a considered strategy.

Analyzing these arrangements is difficult because it is impossible to isolate their effects in relationships as complex as the economic ties among trading nations. Too many other factors simultaneously affect trade, including macroeconomic policies, structural trends, and currency movements. Although it would be a mistake to draw too firm conclusions from U.S. experience, there are useful lessons to be learned.

The FTA with Canada. The free trade agreement with Canada is by far the most ambitious and potentially significant of all the special arrangements into which the United States has entered. It represents a case of two industrial countries, albeit of greatly differing size, living in close proximity and sharing a long history of peaceful relations and a considerable degree of economic integration even before an FTA was attempted. All this makes the U.S.-Canada relationship unique. Also contributing to the unique character of the relationship are the facts that each country is the other's largest trading partner and that more than 70 percent of Canada's exports come to the United States, a proportion that has been growing in recent years.

Because the agreement is just being implemented, all we can assess is its potential. However, that potential is considerable.

The agreement eliminates all remaining tariffs on bilateral trade over a ten-year period and most on a faster timetable. It aims to improve the investment climate in both countries, particularly in Canada, by establishing reciprocal rights and obligations, including a commitment to national treatment. It breaks new ground in setting rules for trade in services by establishing firm contractual obligations on national treatment, on rights of establishment, and on licensing and certification procedures. It opens the financial services sector. And it establishes groundbreaking dispute-settlement procedures.

For all the progress the agreement represents, it fell short of expectations in three areas: The agreement made no substantial progress on subsidies or on intellectual property rights. And despite the success in setting rules on services, there was little liberalization; with the important exceptions of financial services, most existing restrictions were grandfathered in the agreement—that is, left in place and not subjected to the discipline of the new rules. Moreover, it is worth observing that despite the long history of peaceful relations and the considerable degree of economic integration predating the FTA, the negotiations to reach the agreement nearly collapsed on several occasions. Moreover, many Canadians harbored deep misgivings about the implications of the agreement for Canada's political, economic, and cultural autonomy. Canada called an election as a referendum on the FTA, and a majority of Canadians voted for candidates opposed to the agreement. However, a victory of the ruling party (by winning a plurality in a three-way contest) saved it.

Two important lessons emerge from the U.S. experience in negotiating the free trade agreement with Canada. The first lesson is that a bilateral framework is likely to prove inadequate to resolve some issues of vital interest to the United States. The failure of the United States and Canada to reach agreements on subsidies and on intellectual property rights or to achieve significant liberalization of existing barriers to trade in services (outside the financial services sector) was due primarily to the fact that the benefits to be gained in a bilateral trading relationship were not worth the political cost of concessions that would have been required to reach agreement. In potentially sensitive areas such as agriculture, intellectual property, and services, for any single country to gain benefit worth the required concessions, more countries must participate. This is a strong argument in favor of multilateral negotiations to liberalize trade.

The second lesson is that there is no reason on the basis of the Canadian experience to suppose that negotiating FTAs will necessarily be easier or likely to have a greater chance of succeeding than multilateral agreements. In a strictly bilateral setting, the prospect may be even greater that more intense and explosive political considerations will intrude.

In time, other lessons *may* be learned. Once the Uruguay Round is finished, we may learn whether agreements negotiated in a bilateral context can serve as precedents or models for multilateral agreements. Also, if the United States and Canada some day elect to invite other countries to join in their arrangement, we may learn whether bilateral FTAs hold potential as building blocks for broader arrangements. We may also learn whether such agreements trigger a competition among other countries to secure preferential arrangements of their own and contribute to the disintegration of the multilateral, nondiscriminatory trading system.

The FTA with Israel. The U.S.-Israel FTA represents a case of two countries of vastly different sizes, at very different stages of economic development, and separated by great geographic distance. For reasons there is no need to belabor here, the U.S.-Israel relationship, like the U.S. relationship with Canada but for very different reasons, is unique. It is grounded in special historical, political, and strategic circumstances. Were it not for those special circumstances, it is most unlikely that the FTA would ever have been contemplated. When the FTA was concluded in 1985, few took it as a sign of any consequence for the future direction of U.S. trade policy. But it does exist, and experience under it offers some lessons for future U.S. policy.

The U.S.-Israel FTA makes permanent, with minor exceptions, Israel's duty-free access to the U.S. market that Israel enjoyed under the Generalized System of Preferences (GSP). Prior to the agreement, some 90 percent of Israeli exports to the United States were already duty-free, but Israeli officials believed that preferential market access was at risk because the U.S. GSP program was under attack. Congressional critics were also demanding that newly industrializing countries, possibly including Israel some day, be graduated from the program. Beneficiary countries were also increasingly confronted with U.S. demands for concessions as a condition for continued preferences and were hampered by limitations on duty-free access based on competitive need.

Tariffs on U.S. exports to Israel are also reduced or eliminated under the agreement. Israel agreed to liberalize some of its licensing procedures and to sign the GATT codes of conduct on subsidies and on government procurement. Finally, the agreement included a nonbinding commitment to liberalize trade in services with the expectation that these commitments would be made binding in future negotiations.

There is little evidence to date that the agreement (which admittedly is still being implemented) has been either trade-creating or trade-diverting to any significant extent. The growth in Israeli exports to the United States since 1985 is in line with their performance since 1980, and there has been no significant increase in U.S. nonmilitary exports to Israel. Part of the explanation may lie in the fact that U.S. exports to Israel have until now remained subject to nontariff barriers which may have offset the liberalizing effects of tariff reductions. The agreement ignored a major nontariff barrier, Israel's purchase tax and the arbitrary way it has been assessed on imports.[6] However, as a result of recent U.S. representations to Israel, this problem is on the way to resolution; and by 1992, U.S. and Israeli products will receive identical treatment under the purchase tax.

Although the main motives of the United States in entering into the FTA with Israel fall in the realms of international and domestic politics rather than economics, there was one economic consideration: to overcome the disadvantage U.S. products faced entering Israel because of the FTA already in place between Israel and the European Community.

Because of the unique circumstances surrounding it, lessons of broader applicability from the U.S. experience with the FTA with Israel are difficult to draw. One may be that FTA agreements between the United States and very small countries motivated by mainly political considerations are not likely to yield significant economic gains for the United States. Moreover, the fact that a significant Israeli nontariff barrier to the U.S. exports was not touched by the agreement should be a reason to pause when considering agreements that share this profile. Such agreements may not, after all, be a solution to the free-rider problem plaguing multilateral negotiations. Moreover, the prospect of the proliferation of separate bilateral agreements with smaller countries raises questions about the willingness of the United States to monitor and police them effectively. Finally, the fact that the United States had at least some interest in negotiating the FTA to offset an advantage already won by the EC through its own discriminatory arrangements with Israel suggests that other countries may react in similar defensive ways to discriminatory arrangements the United States might negotiate.

The CBI. The Caribbean Basin Initiative (CBI) is an agreement completed in 1983 that extends until 1995, with some significant limitations, one-way, duty-free entry into the United States for the products of a number of very small countries in the Caribbean. It also confers tax benefits on U.S. companies investing in beneficiary countries. The CBI was motivated by a U.S. desire to promote economic growth in an area of substantial political and strategic interest that is burdened with great poverty and threatened with social and political upheaval.

To the extent that the CBI had any economic rationale at all, it was explicitly based on the concept of trade diversion. The idea was to replace U.S. imports from Asia containing little or no U.S. content with imports from the Caribbean containing, it was hoped, significant amounts of U.S. content. Whatever its rationale and motivation, the CBI's economic consequences have been meager.

Sectoral Agreements. The United States is a participant in a growing number of sectoral agreements designed to restrict or manage trade, albeit in some cases in the name of correcting for distortions in the marketplace. It is beyond the scope of this statement to assess fully the implications of these arrangements. Suffice it to say that these sector-focused arrangements governing trade in textiles and apparel (with forty-odd countries), motor vehicles (with Japan), machine tools (with Japan and Taiwan), and steel (with twenty-one countries)[7] are addictive, retard inevitable adjustment to international competition, impose large costs upon the U.S. economy, and offer no useful model for advancing U.S. interests in international trade. They constitute a last resort and not, it is hoped, a permanent retreat from the pressures of adjusting to changing conditions of international competition.

The agreement between the United States and Japan governing trade in semiconductors is conceptually different but no less flawed. It aims to prevent Japanese dumping in the United States *and* in third markets by setting a global floor price for chips and to open the Japanese market to other countries, mainly the United States, by setting a market share target for U.S. semiconductors in Japan. Its objective is to manage trade. It is, in essence, an effort to cope, on a bilateral, product-sector basis, with fundamental differences in the ways in which the U.S. and Japanese economies work—a problem that multilateral rules do not adequately address. The agreement reflects the kind of frustration in U.S.-Japan trade relations that lies at the root of many calls for a bilateral FTA with Japan. The agreement has had the effect of raising semiconductor prices to U.S. industrial consumers, thereby subjecting them to a competitive disadvantage.

Conditional MFN Agreements. Faced with the prospect of reaching no multilateral consensus on issues of high priority during the Tokyo Round of multilateral trade negotiations, the United States and like-minded countries drew up conditional MFN agreements. The agreements, called codes, were structured so that signatory countries enjoyed certain rights relative to other signatories and assumed certain obligations as well. The United States takes the position that countries participating in these codes have no obligation to extend the benefits of the agreements to countries who were not signatories and who did not assume the codes' obligations. (In other words, the United States takes the position that the GATT's most-favored-nation obligation does not apply.) Other countries do not accept the U.S. position, but the issue has not been resolved. The codes, then and now, remain open to any country willing to assume their obligations.

U.S. experience with these plurilateral codes warrants more comprehensive and thorough analysis than it has received to date. The fact that the codes are to a certain extent living documents subject to periodic revision creates challenges for analysts, but more analysis should nevertheless be undertaken.

U.S. Experience with Exceptions: An Outsider's View

The European Community. Although the United States was the main opponent of discriminatory trading arrangements after World War II, there was strong support in the United States for the concept of European economic integration for political and strategic reasons and as a complement to the Marshall Plan. U.S. experience to date relative to the European Community appears to confirm the expectations of economic theory. In the early years of the EC's existence, a substantial volume of trade was diverted from outside countries as a consequence of the discrimination inherent in economic integration. It has been estimated that as much as two-fifths of the rise of internal trade resulted from trade diversion rather than from newly created trade. As time passed, however, and the common external tariffs were reduced, the benefits of European integration spilled over to trade with nonmember countries. The removal of internal trade barriers brought the benefits of economies of scale and specialization as well as the efficiencies associated with a greater degree of competition among the EC's members. These effects were reflected in sharply stepped-up rates of growth in both trade and GNP.

After 1973, the EC's external trade as a proportion of its GNP was actually greater than it had been prior to the establishment of the common market. The trade-diverting effects eventually were overshadowed by the secondary trade-creating consequences of the dynamic forces put into motion by economic integration. The consensus now is that, on balance, the formation of the EC has been a net plus for both the world economy and the United States.

Given its early experience with the consequences of European integration and its experience in the intervening years, the United States is watching the EC's current effort to enhance the scope of its integration—the 1992 process—with a mixture of enthusiasm and anxiety. The 1992 changes portend a quantum jump in the intensity of European integration, ranging from the proposed elimination of border formalities to the substitution of Community-wide quotas for national import quotas, the liberalization of government procurement and trade in services, and the harmonization or mutual recognition of product standards and professional certification. It aims to eliminate all physical, technical, and fiscal barriers to trade among the member states. This means, in short, the creation of the world's largest single market, with a population of 320 million consumers.

What will 1992 mean for the United States? Will the EC become a Fortress Europe, shutting out nonmembers; or will it become a new and more open center of economic dynamism, benefiting not only its members but outsiders as well?

There are worrisome aspects to the integration steps now being considered, such as the substitution of EC-wide formal or informal trade restraints (including restrictive rules of origin) for certain national trade restraints and the imposition of local-content requirements for television programming, motor vehicles, and electronic products. However, the European initiative as a whole should bring substantial benefits to the United States if the integration process is driven by forces of liberalization and openness. For example, by providing a more unified market with harmonized standards and taxes, it should stimulate faster European growth and lead to increased U.S. exports to and investment in the EC.

U.S. policy should actively encourage liberalization and openness in the process of European integration and strongly oppose measures that would take the process in a protectionist, Fortress Europe direction. Specifically, the United States should have four objectives with regard to the 1992 process: (1) to prevent any erosion of the status quo in terms of U.S. access to the EC market, (2) to ensure full national treatment for the European affiliates of U.S. corporations, (3) to work out mutually acceptable arrangements for participation of European and American companies in one another's cooperative research and experimentation projects, and (4) to work with the EC both directly and in the Uruguay Round of multilateral negotiations to ensure that decisions made in the 1992 process are compatible with and supportive of multilateral agreements emerging from the round.

U.S. Trade Policy in the 1990s:
Interests and Options

U.S. Interests

Competing economic and political forces constantly pull U.S. trade policy in opposing directions. Some pull in the direction of more trade and competition governed by the market; others pull in the direction of less trade and competition managed by government policy. In recent years, both paths have led U.S. policy in the direction of negotiating discriminatory trade agreements. For the most part, these agreements have been trade-restrictive; but a few, with apparent growing support, have been trade-liberalizing.

Frustration with the weaknesses of the multilateral system, the experience of the EC, and the promise of the U.S.-Canada Free Trade Agreement all lend support to a shift in U.S. policy toward the negotiation of additional free trade arrangements. Such arrangements could yield benefits for the United States if they succeed in further opening key foreign markets to U.S. exports, establish procedures for resolving disputes in a timely manner, and impose discipline on national policy where no discipline now exists. They could advance the process of trade liberalization at a pace faster than the convoy of trading nations is able to move. And they could tailor U.S. policy to the unique circumstances of important bilateral relationships.

Such arrangements may also produce accords upon which multilateral agreements could later be modeled. They may become building blocks, attracting the participation of a growing number of countries, until they eventually become truly multilateral. Finally, such arrangements may have powerful demonstration effects, proving that it is possible to make progress on complex problems where political will exists and showing the laggards in the trade-liberalization convoy that they cannot indefinitely thwart the progress of others and that by trying to do so, they will be left behind, ultimately to their own considerable disadvantage.

Economic history, the experience of U.S. traders with discriminatory arrangements, and the global scope of U.S. interests offer even better reasons to be highly skeptical that long-term U.S. interests can be adequately served by a policy that emphasizes discriminatory over multilateral, nondiscriminatory arrangements.

There is a strong likelihood that the demonstration effects of a shift in U.S. policy toward discriminatory arrangements would be more powerful than desired and would have consequences detrimental to U.S. interests. It is unrealistic to expect that the United States alone would become the hub of an expanding wheel of such discriminatory arrangements. Regardless of what might be said to the contrary, the unambiguous signal that such a shift in U.S. policy would send to this country's trading partners would be that the United States was abandoning the multilateral trading system.

The policies of other major economic powers, namely the EC and Japan, would unquestionably be affected. European advocates of a Fortress Europe outcome for the 1992 process would be strengthened. Both the EC and Japan would be likely to become hubs themselves as they and, particularly, smaller countries reacted defensively to a perceived major shift in U.S. policy.

World politics in the early 1990s may bear no resemblance to world politics of the late 1930s, but the potential for political friction flowing from centrifugal forces in the world economy is nevertheless real. The risks of misunderstandings, more commercial disputes with stronger political overtones, and increasing mistrust would almost certainly be greater in a trading system dominated by discriminatory arrangements. Moreover, the inevitable result would be a diminution of U.S. power and influence in the world economy and in world politics as well.

The proliferation of networks of preferential arrangements could also introduce complexities and uncertainties into international commerce that ultimately could have a chilling effect on the expansion of world trade. In addition, the imperfect but nevertheless important institutional arrangements now in place, after many decades of consensus building to manage the world trading system, could atrophy.

Running these risks may not be worth even the potential benefits of discriminatory trading arrangements. As the United States discovered in the negotiation of the Free Trade Agreement with Canada, it is likely to prove impossible to reach satisfactory solutions to some problems of highest priority to the United States—including those dealing with services, investment, and intellectual property rights—through bilateral or even plurilateral arrangements with other countries. The main reason is that a critical mass of benefits sufficient to justify economically desirable but politically difficult changes in national policies required to reach agreement is not likely to be achievable with only a limited number of participating countries. Moreover, the outliers (countries that are not parties to such agreements) are likely to be the very countries most in need of international discipline. In addition, as the United States has discovered in living with its agreement with Israel, it may be difficult in bilateral arrangements with smaller countries to construct a framework of mutual concessions that addresses all the obstacles to creating truly free trade. Monitoring and enforcing a large number of preferential and discriminatory arrangements with different terms is likely to be complicated and could require the commitment of more resources than the United States is willing to allocate to the task. Such agreements may not, in the end, solve the free-rider problem. Finally, it may turn out that as the geographic focus of trade negotiations narrows, political and strategic considerations will be more rather than less likely to swamp economic considerations.

We are therefore drawn to two very basic considerations from which our policy recommendations flow. First, the United States has and will continue to have global economic concerns, and it is therefore in the nation's interest to prevent fragmentation of the world economy. Both U.S. global economic interests and U.S. leadership status will be enhanced by the evolution of a stronger multilateral, nondiscriminatory trading system. Despite the relative decline of U.S. economic power and the more equal distribution of power that now characterizes the world economy, there is no country able or willing to replace the United States as the leader of such a system. However, in a world trading system characterized by a network of discriminatory arrangements, several nations could play the role of regional leaders.

This leads us to the conclusion that the highest U.S. trade policy priority for the immediate future must be the successful conclusion of the Uruguay Round of multilateral trade negotiations. There is little prospect of advancing U.S. interests in new international rules for agriculture, safeguards, intellectual property rights, and the distortions caused by trade-related investment measures outside *global* solutions to those problems. A successful conclusion to the Uruguay Round will strengthen the multilateral system, advance the process of trade liberalization, and improve international discipline, thus solving many of the problems that have stimulated interest in discriminatory trading arrangements. Any alternative to multilateral solutions would be a far distant second-best approach.

If the Uruguay Round fails or falls short of achieving U.S. objectives in areas of key importance, the second-best alternative would be arrangements that come as close to multilateral, nondiscriminatory arrangements as possible. That is, the United States should seek to negotiate plurilateral agreements on a global (rather than on a regional) basis that are open to all countries willing to accept the obligations of participation. The United States should preserve the GATT network of obligations but supplement them with agreements that achieve a higher level of trade liberalization with countries that are willing to participate.

Second, although U.S. interests will best be served by a vibrant multilateral and nondiscriminatory trading system, not all regions and countries of the world are of equal importance to us. The United States must, as it always has, differentiate among its trading partners in the formulation and implementation of policy.

Special consideration needs to be given to trade relations with countries of particular importance to the United States, whether because of the magnitude, scope, and intensity of our economic interaction with them (Canada, Japan, the EC); because of our proximity to them and the inevitable linkages among economic, political, security, immigration and other considerations (Mexico, the Caribbean); or because of the special characteristics of certain countries and the large implications of U.S. decisions now for the evolution of the world economy (the dynamic newly industrialized countries of Asia, the heavily indebted middle-income developing countries).

However, it is important to draw a distinction between deciding to differentiate among trading partners and deciding to negotiate discriminatory trading arrangements with them. The case of Japan offers the clearest example of this point: The United States needs a carefully considered policy on trade with Japan, but a free trade agreement with Japan makes no sense. There are other ways to pursue this country's interests in relation to its important trading partners than by entering into discriminatory trading arrangements with them.

Narrowing the Options

Having concluded that multilateral, nondiscriminatory trading arrangements will best serve U.S. interests, and having determined that the second-best alternative would be plurilateral agreements negotiated on a global basis, how desirable are other possible trade policy arrangements?

We strongly recommend against the pursuit of sector-specific arrangements. It may be conceptually possible for such arrangements, whether negotiated bilaterally or among a number of countries, to be motivated by trade-liberalizing intentions and to have trade-liberalizing consequences. The overwhelming experience, however, has been that such managed-trade arrangements are motivated by trade-restricting intentions and have trade-limiting consequences. This tendency has become, regrettably, an increasingly important one in the global economy. It is a course the United States should abandon, not further embrace.

Pacific Rim

The economic dynamism of the Pacific Rim is exciting, and U.S. trade and other economic ties with the region are expanding rapidly. The special characteristics of U.S. trading ties to the Pacific Rim may justify the creation of new forums for consultation and cooperation but not the negotiation of discriminatory trading arrangements. U.S. long-term interests lie in integrating the countries of the Pacific Rim into the global trading system and making them a force for constructing a stronger, more effective multilateral system. U.S. interests do not lie in isolating the countries of the region or in reducing the incentive those countries have to build up the multilateral system. Moreover, given the tremendous diversity of the countries of the region, we are highly skeptical that the United States could succeed in negotiating plurilateral arrangements that would achieve U.S. goals more easily in a Pacific Rim context than in a multilateral context.

Japan

A discriminatory trade agreement negotiated between the United States and Japan (or for that matter between the United States and the European Community) would be fundamentally destructive of the multilateral system and would be most unlikely to resolve the fundamental problems at the root of the perpetual trade friction between the United States and Japan. Were the United States to negotiate such an arrangement with *either* Japan or the EC, the excluded party would find itself in an untenable economic and political position, with potentially adverse long-term economic, geopolitical, and strategic implications.

Proposals to negotiate a free trade agreement with Japan arise out of the frustration and acrimony that characterize U.S.-Japan trade relations. However, two considerations, one macroeconomic and one microeconomic, rule out the negotiation of such an agreement as a solution to the problems in U.S.-Japan trade relations.

The main engine driving the U.S. trade deficit with Japan—without doubt a key source of U.S. frustration in the relationship—is the basic macroeconomic imbalance between the two countries. Until the United States corrects its federal budget deficit, and until both countries bring about a more responsible saving-investment balance within their domestic economies, their huge trade imbalances will persist. Both countries' governments know what they must do to correct the macroeconomic foundation of their bilateral and global imbalances. In recent years, it is Japan that has shown greater will and ability to act responsibly on this issue, but neither government has done enough. No bilateral agreement governing commercial policy can solve the problem that lies at the root of this issue: the fear of the political leadership in both countries that their electorates are unprepared to make the adjustments that need to be made.

A bilateral free trade agreement would not be able to address successfully the microeconomic sources of tension in the trading relationship. The barriers to enhanced Japanese access to the U.S. market are relatively clear: tariffs (such as the U.S. 25 percent duty on light trucks), quotas (mainly voluntary agreements restraining Japanese exports of autos, steel, and machine tools), and the exposure of Japanese exports to attack under the various U.S. unfair trade statutes. These barriers are transparent and are obviously the product of U.S. government policy. They are amenable to change by government policy as a result of international agreements.

The barriers to enhanced U.S. access to the Japanese market also include tariffs (e.g., on wood products) and quotas (e.g., as on rice) that are relatively straightforward and are the product of government policy. But characteristics inherent in the way Japan's economy is organized and operates also constitute barriers. They encompass aspects of Japan's industrial structure, business practices, legal system, and financial structure, and they tend to place foreign producers (and sometimes even *Japanese* newcomers to a particular market) at a competitive disadvantage. These barriers are the product of the long evolution of Japan's business culture and society, and there are severe limits on the extent to which government policy can affect them, particularly in the short term. As we mentioned earlier, we believe that these are best dealt with by a strong combination of business-to-business and government-to-government negotiations, as outlined in *Strengthening U.S.-Japan Economic Relations: An Action Program for the Public and Private Sectors,* a 1989 joint statement by CED and its Japanese counterpart organization, Keizai Doyukai.

Mexico

Mexico, without doubt, deserves special consideration in the context of U.S. trade policy. It is this country's third-largest trading partner. Economic integration between Mexico and the United States is substantial and growing steadily. Moreover, Mexico is in the midst of a dramatic, highly positive shift in economic policy, turning a traditionally closed, autarchic economy into one increasingly open to trade and investment from the rest of the world.

These facts alone would justify giving special consideration to Mexico. But there is, of course, much more to the bilateral relationship. Nearly $20 billion of Mexico's more than $100 billion external debt is owed to U.S. financial institutions. How Mexico and the United States manage these debt obligations while making it possible for Mexico to resume economic growth after six years of austerity will have a large impact on the course of the overall problem of developing country debt. Moreover, the two countries share a 2,000-mile border, and across that border flow scores of Mexican immigrants, many illegal, and much of the illicit drugs entering the United States. That border means the United States has a huge stake in the evolution of a peaceful, prosperous, and politically stable Mexico. There is no way the United States can isolate its commercial relations in this larger setting.

For decades until quite recently, U.S.-Mexico trade relations were characterized by conflict and mistrust, but the past four years have brought about major change. Beginning in 1985, Mexico turned away from its traditional policy of economic autarchy and import substitution and embarked on a course of unilateral liberalization. Within a short time, Mexico joined the GATT, resolved a long-standing dispute with the United States over subsidies, concluded a framework agreement with the United States providing for consultations and dispute settlement, and entered into a new understanding that is expected to lead to further agreements liberalizing trade and investment. Mexico has also begun a vigorous program of domestic economic deregulation and is eliminating many obstacles to foreign direct investment. As a result, U.S.-Mexico trade and investment relations are better today than at any time in memory. Problems abound, but mistrust and acrimony have been replaced by a businesslike approach and considerable good will on both sides.

The U.S.-Mexico Framework Agreement consists of three elements: (1) a statement of principle that emphasizes the importance to both countries of an "open and predictable environment for international trade and investment"; (2) a special procedure for consultations and dispute settlement, including a timetable, before problems are referred to the GATT; and (3) an action agenda which commits both governments to consultations on a range of product-sector matters. In substance, the agreement is modest. In the context of the history of U.S.-Mexican trade relations, it constitutes a major achievement.

The U.S.-Mexico Understanding Regarding Trade and Investment Facilitation Talks mandates trade and investment negotiations between the two countries and opens the door to improved trade relations. It establishes a negotiating process and sets a specific timetable for the selection of issues to be negotiated and for negotiations themselves. While the understanding does not itself create more trade and investment, it sets in motion a process that should make both possible. Moreover, coincident with the approval of the Understanding, the two governments reached agreements to expand Mexican steel exports to the United States and to improve the protection of intellectual property rights in Mexico.

The framework agreement and the U.S.-Mexico Understanding reflect the reality acknowledged by both governments that market forces are inexorably pushing the two countries toward closer economic integration. The question for governments is how to shape and influence the course of this integration. It is in that context that the question arises of what further institutional arrangements between the United States and Mexico, if any, make sense?

Political leaders in both countries agree that the obstacles to the negotiation of a formal free trade agreement between the United States and Mexico in any short time frame are probably insurmountable. The two countries' levels of economic development are too disparate. Equally important, the politics of such a proposal in both countries, but particularly in Mexico, would be potentially explosive. Fears of U.S. domination are still very much alive. Such a proposal, particularly if initiated by the United States, could set off a controversy in Mexico that would make the rancorous debate in Canada over approval of the U.S.-Canada Free Trade Agreement appear tame.

Alternative approaches can be taken. The two governments can continue to address issues on an ad hoc basis as they arise in a way that would advance the process of economic integration without trying to define an ultimate goal. An alternative would be to enter into negotiations aimed at achieving a comprehensive free trade agreement over an extended period of time, with a differential pace of liberalization reflecting the two countries' different levels of economic development. Concrete proposals for such negotiations have been made[8] and deserve serious consideration. However, given the political sensitivity of the relationship, the United States should defer to Mexico to take the initiative for any negotiations of this type.

As the process proceeds, the United States needs to be sensitive to the implications for trade with Canada, which is already a free trade partner of the United States. Whenever discussion of economic integration with Mexico is seriously considered, thought should be given to approaching the subject in terms of a free trade agreement on a North American scale involving all three countries.

Notes

1. Multilateralism is the practice of taking a collective or universal approach to negotiating trade arrangements, rather than negotiating them on a country-by-country or regional basis. Nondiscrimination refers to the policy of treating all trading partners equally. In referring to multilateralism in this statement, we intend to encompass the concept of nondiscrimination as well.

2. The MFN principle is embodied in paragraph 1 of Article I of the GATT. It provides that each signatory country must extend to all other signatories any advantage in trade it confers upon its "most favored" trading partner. In

the words of the Agreement: "any advantage, favor, privilege, or immunity granted by any contracting party . . . shall be accorded immediately and unconditionally to . . . all other contracting parties."

3. Notable exceptions include, for example, the 25 percent tariff the United States levies on imported trucks, the 20 percent tariff imposed by the EC on footwear, and Japan's 20 percent tariff on some laminated wood products.

4. See, for example, Paul Wannacott and Mark Lutz, eds., "Is There a Case for Free Trade Areas?" in *Free Trade Areas and U.S. Trade Policy* (Washington, D.C.: Institute for International Economics, 1989), pp. 59–84.

5. The members include Norway, Sweden, Iceland, Finland, Austria, and Switzerland.

6. See Howard F. Rosen, "The U.S.-Israel Free Trade Area Agreement: How Well Is It Working and What Have We Learned?" in *Free Trade Areas and U.S. Trade Policy,* pp. 97–120. See also Joseph Pelzman, "Sweetheart Deal," *The International Economy* (March–April 1989), pp. 53–56.

7. The bilateral restrictions in steel are justified mainly on the basis of foreign subsidization of steel.

8. See, for example, *Options for Liberalizing U.S.-Mexico Trade and Investment.* (Mexico City and Washington, D.C.: Mexico-U.S. Business Committee, June 1989).

5

Trade and Investment

Foreign trade and international investment are inextricably linked. Both are mechanisms by which nations optimize the use of their resources. And both have expanded far more rapidly in recent years than national production. The resulting integration of the global economy has brought immeasurable benefits worldwide, but it has also led to international strains and conflict.

Despite the close links between trade and investment, there is a fundamental asymmetry in the way the two are treated internationally. GATT is a multilateral institution for promoting trade liberalization, a common set of trade rules, and an instrument for resolving trade disputes between nations. The ongoing Uruguay Round is a major effort to enlarge the scope of GATT (especially by including trade in services) and to strengthen it in relation to all three of its functions.

Nothing comparable exists for international investment.[1] In that field, the United States is party to a number of bilateral investment treaties as well as a "soft law" arrangement in the form of nonmandatory guidelines for multinational enterprises applying to OECD members. In addition, the United States has been a participant in a long, desultory, and still unfinished exercise in the United Nations intended to develop a universal code of conduct for transnational corporations. An entirely separate organization is the World Bank's International Centre for the Settlement of Investment Disputes (ICSID). On average, it has handled little more than one case a year since its inception in 1966. This patchwork of intergovernmental arrangements hardly qualifies as a coordinated regime for international investment.

In light of the increasing internationalization of business, including new forms of intercorporate alliances that mix national identities, the question arises of whether the time has come to consider a more integrated approach in the form of a GATT for investment. Like GATT, such an agreement could combine a binding set of rules on investment, a dispute-settlement facility, and a mechanism for liberalizing national policies and regulations regarding foreign enterprise.

Links Between Trade and Investment

General

At the macroeconomic level, net international flows of capital are simply the counterpart of national imbalances in trade in goods and services (essentially the current balance-of-payment account):[2] A trade-surplus country is a net capital exporter; a trade-deficit country is a net capital importer. Most international movement of capital consists of financial flows rather than direct investment in the sense of the acquisition of a controlling interest in a new or ongoing foreign enterprise. However, some of the main recent trends in direct investment have coincided with shifts in the location of world current-account imbalances: The emergence of the United States as the major host country and Japan as a major home country for direct foreign investment has paralleled their roles as the world's principal trade deficit and surplus countries, respectively.

At the microeconomic level, the links between trade and investment are obvious. If a U.S. exporter establishes a plant abroad, it may no longer export the products produced by that plant. Or the foreign affiliate may produce components of the product which the parent company then imports into the United States, assembles, and exports as before. Many possibilities exist. But the decision to open a plant abroad would be affected by the host country's regulations on foreign investment. They could encourage foreign investment—for example, by providing tax incentives; or they could discourage it—for example, by mandating majority local ownership.

Just as national investment policies affect the flow of trade, national trade policies affect the international flow of investment. The imposition of severe restrictions on imports or arbitrary rules of origin may impel a foreign exporter to establish a local production facility to serve the sheltered domestic market. For example, actual or feared protection has been a major factor motivating Japanese investment in U.S. automotive production. Similarly, U.S.-induced voluntary export restraints on textiles and clothing may have stimulated stepped-up Japanese investment in Asian developing countries less affected by the export restraints. Another example is the European rule of origin applying to semiconductors, which has the effect of inducing investment in the European Community.

Perhaps the best reflection of the intimate linkage between trade and investment is the major role that multinational companies play in world trade. Approximately half of world exports of nonagricultural products originates in companies that are units in a multinational network, while about a quarter consists of exchanges between units of individual multinational firms.

U.S. Policy Initiatives

In recent years, the United States has implicitly acknowledged the close links between trade and investment in a number of specific policy initiatives.

Because services have become so vital a part of the domestic and international economy,[3] the United States insisted on including the liberalization of trade in services in the Uruguay Round. It took a strong position that commitments would be necessary not only with respect to the usual border restrictions on trade but also with respect to rights of establishment for U.S. service enterprises abroad and their treatment once established. Without such assurances (including national and non-discriminatory treatment), trade liberalization for service industries, such as banking and insurance, would be meaningless, since the bulk of the foreign sales of such services can, as a practical matter, be accomplished only through an established presence in the foreign country.

Another U.S. initiative linking trade and investment in the Uruguay Round is the agenda item on trade-related investment measures. In this case, the United States is seeking to limit the conditions imposed on foreign investors in the form of local-content requirements and export targets that have restrictive and distorting effects on trade. Rules on this subject are regarded by the U.S. government as an initial step toward the longer-run goal of a comprehensive international investment agreement.*

The U.S.-Canada Free Trade Agreement also illustrates the growing recognition of the close links between trade and investment. The agreement includes commitments not only to remove trade barriers between the two countries but also to liberalize conditions for foreign investment. It provides national treatment for the establishment, acquisition, and conduct of businesses and bans the imposition of most performance requirements imposed on foreign investments.

A final example of an ad hoc U.S. investment policy initiative in the context of a trade development relates to the European Community's

---

*See memorandum by Edmund T. Pratt, Jr. (p. 139).

moves toward a single market by 1992. In the early stages of EC decision making on 1992, it appeared that the Community would not accord national treatment to foreign enterprises in the financial services sector. Instead, the draft Second Banking Directive would have applied the reciprocity principle—that is, foreign enterprises would receive the same treatment in the Community that EC enterprises were accorded in the foreign country. This principle implied that in order for a foreign financial services enterprise to receive national treatment in the Community, its home country would be required to adopt the identical laws and regulations that governed in the Community, clearly an untenable condition.

After strong representations from both the U.S. government and private sector, the EC Commission—and the Council of Ministers—have now proposed a more acceptable two-track approach that appears likely to survive through the imminent final stages of the political process: (1) The EC will continue to pursue its objective of "effective market access" to foreign markets comparable to what the EC grants in its own market but will do so through bilateral negotiations independent of the licensing procedures; (2) licensing of subsidiaries of non-EC parent enterprises will be held up only in those cases where the home country fails to grant national treatment to EC enterprises. Once established in the EC, subsidiaries of non-EC enterprises receive the full benefits of the "single banking license."

Concerns About Foreign Investment

These U.S. initiatives are part of a continuing process of carrying out the policy on international investment enunciated by the White House in a major statement issued in 1983. Its basic principle is that "foreign investment flows which respond to private market forces will lead to more efficient international production and thereby benefit both home and host countries."[4]

However, the proposition that the free flow of foreign direct investment (FDI) is in the U.S. national interest is not universally accepted. Questions have been raised about the effects of FDI on the United States both as home and as host country. With the soaring volume of inward direct investment in recent years, the questioning has become particularly insistent with respect to U.S. policies as host country.

Inward Investment

Between 1980 and 1988, the stock of FDI in the United States multiplied fourfold, compared with an increase of only 50 percent in the stock of U.S. direct investment abroad.[5] Of the total 1988 stock of $329 billion of FDI in the United States, Europe accounted for 66 percent and Japan for only 16 percent. However, the rate of growth of FDI originating in Japan has outstripped the flows from Europe over the past eight years. At present, about half of Japanese direct investment abroad takes place in the United States.

Japanese direct investment in the United States has been heavy in banking and finance, commerce, real estate, and manufacturing. Protectionist measures and sentiment against imports of manufactured products from Japan have been important reasons for the Japanese desire to serve the U.S. market from production within this country. Until recently, Japanese companies have tended to establish wholly owned green-field investments rather than purchase existing enterprises. However, acquisitions and mergers have risen rapidly since 1985, stimulated by the sharp appreciation of the yen in the 1985–1988 period.[6]

The steep increase in inflows of foreign direct investment in recent years has given rise to fears of the "buying up" of America by foreigners. Concerns expressed about the loss of control of our own economic destiny echo the cries heard over the years in Canada and many developing countries about the impact of U.S. investment in those countries.

However, the subject needs to be placed in perspective. At the end of 1988, U.S. companies' investments in their foreign affiliates ($327 billion) were almost equal to foreign direct investment in this country ($329). Moreover, because the statistics are based on book rather than market value, they understate the comparative value of U.S. FDI, which is on average of older vintage than foreign investment in the United States. The understatement is reflected in the fact that earnings on U.S. direct investment abroad in 1988 ($52 billion) were more than four times the earnings on foreign direct investment in this country ($12 billion).[7]

A more basic point is that the net inflow of capital from abroad in all forms is simply the counterpart of the U.S. deficit in its current account. Therefore, the inflow can be reduced only by narrowing that deficit. An essential condition for reducing the external deficit is the narrowing of the gap between U.S. income and the sum of U.S. public and private expenditures. So long as the gap persists, the United States will be drawing on capital from abroad. Under present circumstances, therefore, the question is not whether this country wants or does not want foreign investment but rather the form in which the inflow of capital is to take place.

Most of the inflow of capital to the U.S. is invested in liquid financial assets. Of total foreign private assets in the U.S. at the end of 1987 amounting to $1,253 billion, only $262 billion, or 21 percent, took the form of direct investment.[8] From the standpoint of limiting volatility in financial markets, it is surely better to have a share of the U.S. current-account deficit financed by direct investment, implying a long-term commitment to the U.S. economy, than entirely through the acquisition by foreigners of liquid financial assets. A sudden large liquidation of foreign assets could have highly adverse effects on the U.S. economy by sharply weakening the dollar and exerting strong upward pressure on interest rates.

Apart from contributing to financial stability, foreign direct investment in the United States brings the benefits that this country, as the world's largest investor abroad, has long cited as advantages for the host country. These are the increased output generated by the transfer of additional productive resources to the United States in the form of capital, technology, and management. The rewards of the increased output will accrue not only to the foreign investor in the form of profits but also to domestic labor in the form of increased wages and to the country as a whole in the form of improved technology and skills and larger tax revenues for the government. Moreover, the direct participation in American business by internationally oriented European and Japanese companies may improve U.S. export performance by opening up new marketing opportunities abroad for products manufactured in America. Directly or indirectly, the increased production resulting from the investment should generate the foreign exchange required to remit the profits to the foreign investors. Finally, as with international trade, foreign direct investment sharpens competition in the U.S. market, thereby stimulating greater efficiency and improved quality for domestic production.

Subsidies. Although the foregoing considerations argue strongly in favor of preserving the present U.S. policy of openness to foreign direct investment, two qualifying considerations need to be taken into account. The first relates to subsidies. It is understandable that domestic firms would be concerned about competing in the U.S. market against foreign-owned companies that may be the beneficiaries of special government incentives. Although foreign investors are treated much the same as American firms as far as federal incentives are concerned, they are sometimes singled out for special treatment as recipients of subsidies at the state level. State incentives to attract foreign investment have included generous packages of benefits such as assistance for site selection, low-interest loans, tax holidays, employee training, and special schools for the children of employees.[9]

We support the principle of national treatment for foreign investment. However, special subsidies limited to foreign firms go beyond national treatment. They distort the international flow of capital and create a competitive disadvantage for domestic firms. They should be discouraged as part of a broader effort to negotiate a new international code of conduct for foreign direct investment.

Security. A second qualifying consideration relates to national security. Congressional concern about the national security implications of foreign investment was sparked by the proposed purchase in 1988 of Fairchild Semiconductor Corporation by Fujitsu, Ltd., of Japan. Prior to the enactment of the Omnibus Trade and Competitiveness Act of 1988, there was no law in force explicitly authorizing the prevention of takeovers of U.S. firms by foreign companies when national security concerns were raised. Section 5021 of the act (the Exon-Florio Amendment) addresses this problem by giving the President authority, if he makes certain findings, to prevent foreign acquisitions that threaten to impair U.S. national security. The law requires an investigation to determine the effect of the foreign control on national security and provides guidance as to what considerations to take into account in making the determination.

National security is sometimes invoked as a pretext for imposing obstacles to foreign investment. Section 5021 of the trade act provides a reasonable approach to satisfying legitimate national security concerns while preserving an open policy toward foreign acquisitions and mergers.

However, the recently proposed Treasury regulations for implementing the new law are excessively broad, uncertain in their application, and potentially retroactive. Such uncertainties are an extra deterrent to foreign investment. The regulations in effect require detailed information in the case of foreign takeovers in all industries except toys and games, food products, hotels and restaurants, and legal services.[10] We believe a narrower interpretation would serve the purposes of the statute without imposing unnecessarily burdensome requirements on foreign investors.

Outward Investment

Concerns in the United States about foreign direct investment are not confined to inward flows. Fears have been expressed that American investment abroad leads to the loss of production, jobs, and exports for the U.S. economy.

The worry applies especially to manufacturing, where it is often assumed that in the absence of the U.S. investment abroad, the production would have remained at home. However, that alternative is not realistic. Much of U.S. investment in manufacturing abroad is intended to serve the host-country market. In some cases, it is induced by foreign import barriers; in others, the motivation may be to avoid high transport costs, adapt products more easily to local tastes and requirements, or achieve more efficient integration of production, marketing, and after-sale servicing. Generally, the alternative of manufacturing at home and exporting to the foreign market does not exist. As Oren Shaffer, Chief Financial Officer of the Goodyear Tire and Rubber Company, recently put it, "If you really want to be a player, you have to be inside foreign markets."[11]

If American firms do not establish affiliates abroad to serve local markets, the chances are that firms based in other industrial countries will. Thus, the displacement of U.S. jobs or exports does not normally occur. Rather, U.S.-owned manufacturing facilities catering to a host-country market support U.S. jobs to the extent that they are substantial purchasers of U.S. capital goods and parent-company parts and components. According to the Commerce Department, about 30 percent of the nation's total exports in recent years has consisted of shipments from U.S. parent companies to their foreign subsidiaries.[12]

Similar reasoning applies to direct investment abroad primarily for export back to the United States or to third countries. To the extent that such investment occurs because of a fundamental shift in cost advantages to other countries (e.g., shoe production in developing countries), the continuation of production in the United States on the same scale as before would not be viable. Worker displacement from particular jobs does occur, and programs should be instituted to facilitate adjustment to other jobs more in keeping with U.S. comparative advantage. The alternative of protecting our noncompetitive sectors would be a costly and inefficient way of dealing with the problem.

Over the long run, U.S. workers stand to gain both directly and indirectly from U.S. investment abroad in response to lower-cost foreign opportunities. Domestic jobs are upgraded as workers move from older, less competitive industries to new, more sophisticated ones. In addition, labor gains from favorable feedback to the U.S. economy; U.S. investments abroad increase foreign incomes, some of which are spent on imports from the United States; and remitted earnings are available for new investment in the more advanced sectors of the American economy, where wages are higher.

On the other hand, when the foreign competitive advantage is due to an overvalued dollar or to subsidies paid by foreign governments, the relocation of American manufacturing facilities abroad represents a distortion in the allocation of resources. In such circumstances, however rational the move may be from the perspective of the individual company, it is uneconomic and disruptive from the standpoint of society as a whole and imposes costly adjustments, particularly on American labor. The remedy lies not in treating the symptoms of the problem by restricting the outflow of U.S. investment but in vigorously addressing the underlying causes.

National Policies on Foreign Investment

General Trends

In recent years, there has been a marked trend toward the liberalization of policies on foreign direct investment in both developed and developing countries. Despite the large structural imbalances in the international accounts of the developed countries, controls on FDI have not been used as a major means of dealing with them. Instead, the main reliance has been on macroeconomic adjustments through fiscal, monetary, and foreign exchange policies. However, foreign trade measures have also been resorted to, and these have had important secondary effects on the flows of FDI.

In developing countries, the traditional policy of confrontation has been largely replaced by a pragmatic approach and active encouragement of inflows of FDI. The old attitude of inevitable conflict has given way in most countries to an understanding of the mutual benefits that can result from cooperation between host governments and foreign enterprise.[13]

The Industrial Countries

Outward investment from the major industrial countries is today substantially free of home-government controls. Those residual controls that exist are of little significance.[14] The main current concern of governments with respect to outward investment is to ensure fair treatment for home-based multinational firms in their foreign operations. For example, the United States has invoked the Super 301 provision of the Omnibus Trade and Competitiveness Act as a means of inducing a liberalization of the burdensome performance requirements placed by India on foreign investors.

Inward investment, however, has long been subject to control, and a number of countries have retained their screening requirements for the purpose of protecting national economic and political interests from the impact of multinational firms. Although the criteria and procedures for screening have in most cases been liberalized (e.g., in Canada), some domestic sectors such as transport, shipping, and broadcasting remain closed to FDI in most industrial countries.

The U.S. Omnibus Trade and Competitiveness Act of 1988 authorizes the President to prevent foreign acquisitions that threaten to impair the national security. Responsibility for administering the new law has been vested in the interagency Committee on Foreign Investment in the United States (CFIUS) chaired by the Treasury Department. Although the committee was notified of almost 100 cases during the first year after the act was passed, it agreed to recommend blocking an acquisition in only one case.[15] In general, the United States remains wide open to foreign investment and accords such investment national treatment.

Perhaps the major trend in the United States has been the effort to integrate worldwide policies concerning foreign direct investment, foreign trade in goods and services, and intellectual property protection. This effort has been pursued through U.S. initiatives in the Uruguay Round, in the U.S.-Canada Free Trade Agreement, and in the representations made to the European Community in relation to the move toward a single European market by 1992.

Although the European move is primarily one of *internal* liberalization and dismantlement of controls, it is already having profound effects in stimulating not only intra-EC investment but substantial inflows of *external* investment as well. In addition, initial concerns about the possibility of discriminatory treatment of foreign firms in the banking field have been largely allayed.

The general trend toward liberalization in the EC has also had the effect of slowing down efforts to impose controls on multinational companies at the Community level. In their original forms, these controls would have consisted of burdensome requirements for disclosure of information and consultations with employees (the Vredeling Directive) and employee participation in decision making (Fifth Company Law Directive). Negotiations on these measures stagnated for some time. However, at EC Commission President Delors's initiative, and with the EC Parliament's shift to the left in the mid-1989 election, debate on a broad EC social dimension has now resumed. Opponents, such as the U.K. government, are trying to ensure that as much as possible is left to member states to decide at the national level.

Outward investment from Japan appears to be substantially free of any government approval requirement since enactment of the Foreign Exchange and Foreign Trade Control Law of 1980.[16] However, the surge of Japanese foreign investment has been less a consequence of Japanese government policies than of the strong yen and the effort to preserve markets abroad in the face of actual or threatened protection.

The situation with respect to inward investment is less clear. In order to encourage it, Japan's Ministry of International Trade and

Industry (MITI) created an office for the promotion of foreign investment, as well as special financing facilities to provide foreign investors with loans at favorable rates. However, the acquisition of existing Japanese companies by foreign firms still appears to be informally discouraged despite the absence of any legal barriers to foreign takeovers.

Developing Countries

Changes over the past five years in the laws and regulations of developing countries have confirmed the trend toward the liberalization of inward foreign investment that became apparent in the early 1980s. The conflicted attitude of individual host developing countries toward foreign enterprise has always been reflected in a mixture of measures designed, on the one hand, to encourage FDI and, on the other, to control it. In recent years, the greater emphasis has been on efforts to encourage it by reducing restrictions and requirements and by offering various guarantees and incentives.

This change can be ascribed to a number of factors. First, there has been a slowdown in economic growth and a sharp drop in the level of investment in relation to GNP in many developing countries during the 1980s. To the extent that the improvement of investment rates is seen as essential to more rapid growth, the objections to FDI lose much of their force. Second, because of slow growth, most of the developing countries have become less attractive as locations for foreign enterprise. They have, therefore, adopted special measures to induce it. Third, the technological gap between developing and developed countries has widened, and the realization of the vital role that FDI can play in narrowing the gap has grown.

Fourth, and most important, the burden of foreign debt is being felt in most developing countries. Servicing the debt retards growth by limiting the resources available for capital formation and for imports of essential goods and services. With new private commercial lending virtually dried up, FDI plays a vital role in relieving the capital shortage. For example, in 1987, direct investment from OECD countries accounted for two-thirds of total private resource flows to developing countries.[17]

Moreover, the debt crisis dealt a blow to the conventional wisdom that commercial borrowing had the advantage of providing unencumbered resources in contrast with the foreign control over local enterprise inherent in direct investment. Developing countries discovered that in the end, borrowing resulted in more, not less, external intervention. When debt-repayment schedules could not be met, countries had no effective alternative but to submit to severe austerity programs as the condition for debt rescheduling and International Monetary Fund emergency financing. The alleged problem of foreign control over this or that local enterprise receded in the wake of the far-reaching economic, social, and political consequences of externally negotiated conditionality.

Despite the broad liberalization of Third World policies toward FDI, the developing countries have not abandoned the principle that the entry and operation of multinational firms should be subject to some degree of control to ensure their compatibility with national objectives. Thus, the institutional arrangements for registering and authorizing FDI have generally remained in effect, but with various administrative improvements and simplifications. Performance requirements remain widespread, but willingness to refer investment disputes to international arbitration is gaining ground.

Key Issues

The current improved climate for foreign investment makes this a propitious time for concerted international action to consolidate the gains already achieved and to seek agreement on a set of rules to reduce the remaining distortions and discriminations in the treatment of foreign investment. A number of key issues will need to be addressed.

Right of Establishment

Limits on the right to establish foreign enterprises take a number of forms. Certain sensitive sectors of economic activity may be reserved to enterprises owned wholly or in part by nationals of the host country. Limits may also be set on foreign takeovers of existing domestic enterprises. And some developing countries have adopted "fade-out" provisions requiring the eventual withdrawal of foreign investors from domestic enterprises in which they participate.

The United States is an example of a country that restricts foreign investment in certain sectors—for example, telecommunications, shipping, and nuclear power. In addition, many states restrict foreign investment in banking and insurance, and the President may prevent any takeover that threatens to impair the national security.

A major obstacle to achieving international agreement on rights of establishment is the need to define what constitutes a legitimate policy reason for restricting foreign investment. Recognizing that some limits on the scope of foreign enterprise will continue, we believe such restrictions should be applied on a most-favored-nation basis (i.e., equal treatment for foreign firms regardless of their nationality). Because administrative procedures for screening can themselves be a major deterrent to foreign investment, governments should provide greater clarity in the rules and streamlined procedures for clearances and licenses.

National Treatment

National treatment is the principle that foreign investors, once established in a country, should be treated no less favorably than domestic enterprises with respect to national laws, regulations and administrative practices. The United States applies this principle in its treatment of foreign enterprises, but departures from it are substantial in many countries, particularly in the developing world.

Even the EC initially considered applying the principle of reciprocity rather than national treatment in its 1992 directive on foreign investment in the financial services industry. Its revised position is still not that of unconditional national treatment espoused by the United States but, rather, one of conditioning its national treatment of the foreign enterprise on the latter's home government providing national (but not necessarily identical) treatment to EC enterprises.

We endorse the staunch U.S. advocacy of the principle of unconditional national treatment. However, the principle is far from an ironclad guarantee of nondiscrimination. Certain types of regulations, such as limitations on the remittance abroad of profits, may nominally apply to domestic as well as foreign firms, but their impact is overwhelmingly discriminatory in practice. Such discriminatory practices should be eliminated.

Performance Requirements

These are conditions imposed by host governments on the entry or operation of foreign enterprises. They encompass a wide variety of measures, such as local-content requirements, minimum export levels, technology-transfer obligations, and licensing requirements. By pressuring firms toward economic behavior inconsistent with market forces, they directly or indirectly distort trade and investment flows, lead to uneconomic use of resources, and harm the interests of other countries. These effects are most pronounced in the case of export obligations and local-content requirements.

Minimum export obligations artificially increase exports. They may displace another country's home production or its sales to third markets. Producers can usually recoup losses on the uneconomic exports by exploiting protected positions in the host-country market. Local-content requirements artificially reduce imports by mandating that a given percentage of the value of the final product be produced locally or purchased from local sources. Often, the two types of obligations are combined in trade-balancing requirements that link a firm's permitted imports to the value of its exports so that no net foreign exchange costs are incurred.

Performance requirements should be made subject to clear international discipline so that those demonstrably damaging to other countries' interests are avoided or removed. At U.S. initiative, these practices are on the agenda of the Uruguay Round of GATT negotiations, but progress in reaching an agreement has been slow.

Pending the adoption of explicit international rules on the broad range of performance requirements, the United States should vigorously counter export and local-content requirements bilaterally under existing GATT rules (Articles III, XI, and XVI) whenever they adversely affect U.S. interests.

Incentives and Disincentives

Investment incentives and disincentives are closely related to performance requirements. They are, in fact, the principal mechanism for enforcing such requirements. Foreign enterprises that do not comply may be barred from a host country or subject to various penalties. Conversely, companies willing to adhere to performance requirements may be offered incentives, such as tax concessions or low-interest loans.

Even when not linked to performance requirements, government incentives and subsidies to attract foreign direct investment distort international flows of capital and, indirectly, international trade as well. GATT recognizes that domestic subsidies may be legitimate instruments for achieving certain national social and economic objectives. But the subsidies should be available on a nondiscriminatory basis to firms within a country regardless of the nationality of their ownership. Competition among countries in offering special inducements to attract foreign investment can be a costly negative-sum game.

The only multilateral undertaking on this subject is the Decision of the OECD Council on International Incentives and Disincentives, originally adopted in 1976 and subsequently revised. Unfortunately, it does not go very far. It merely provides for consultations "at the request of a member country which considers that its interests may be adversely affected by the impact on its flow of international direct investments of measures taken by another member country which provide significant official incentives and disincentives to international direct investment." The purpose of the consultations is to "examine the possibility of reducing such effects to a minimum."

It is doubtful that this weak OECD decision has had any material deterrent impact on the use of special inducements to attract foreign direct investment. An effort to craft a more effective international instrument on incentives should be part of any general attempt to negotiate a multilateral convention on foreign direct investment.

Controls on Remittance of Income

Many developing countries place restrictions on the remittance of profits as well as royalties and fees on the transfer of technology. In some countries, the controls are part of their permanent direct investment policies under which permitted remittances may be limited to a portion of the firm's foreign exchange earnings or subject to additional taxation. In other countries, income can be transferred abroad without special limitations except for temporary restrictions applied as part of broader exchange controls during periods of serious external imbalance. Such emergency measures have proliferated as a result of the debt-servicing problems of many developing countries and in some cases have been superimposed on the permanent restrictions.

Limitations on remittances are major deterrents to new inflows of foreign investment. Moreover, they have other unfortunate effects. They encourage disguised remittances in the form of artificial transfer prices in transactions between affiliates of a multinational firm. As a result, the host country's share of taxes on profits may be reduced. In addition, where dividends are subject to greater restrictions than interest payments, encouragement is given to excessive proportions of debt to equity in the foreign enterprise's capital structure.

Early liberalization and ultimate elimination of the restrictions on remittances would serve the interests of the developing countries. It would reduce a major obstacle to new inflows of FDI at a time when private commercial lending has virtually ceased for many debt-ridden developing countries desperately in need of additional capital to restore acceptable rates of economic growth.

Nationalization, Compensation, and Dispute Settlement

The threat of expropriation was a major deterrent to foreign investment in the developing countries prior to the 1980s. Emerging after World War II from colonialism and without experience or training for dealing with foreign enterprises, the newly independent nations were highly suspicious of global corporations. Their fears were seemingly confirmed by the well-publicized role of a multinational corporation in destabilizing the Allende regime in Chile during the early 1970s. However atypical that episode, it served to intensify the hostility toward foreign enterprise and to legitimize widespread acts of expropriation, many of them more as public demonstrations of political sovereignty than as considered economic measures.

Evidence of changing Third World attitudes toward foreign enterprise can be discerned in the dramatic decline in acts of expropriation after 1975. The eighty-three expropriations in that year marked the peak of a rising trend of nationalizations during the preceding decade and a half. In the period from 1970 to 1975, an average of fifty-six expropriations took place each year. In contrast, the number of such acts during the 1980–1985 period averaged fewer than three per year.[18]

The declining salience of the nationalization issue also reflects more fundamental developments than changes in Third World attitudes and policies toward foreign enterprise. In contrast with earlier periods when state ownership was expanding, the current trend is the reverse, especially in Asia and Latin America. In sectors as diverse as steel, railroads, petroleum, banking, and telecommunications, extensive privatization programs have been announced in order to improve efficiency, increase innovation, and stem the drain of public resources.

Another development contributing to the declining importance of the expropriation issue is the change in the nature of the multinational corporation itself. In recent years, there has been a sharp decline in the dominant role of U.S. multinationals in the Third World relative to those from other home bases, including rising numbers of foreign enterprises based in other developing countries. There has also been an increasing trend toward intercorporate alliances of mixed nationality and a growing number of management contracts and other arrangements in which equity ownership is not the key element of control. All these changes weaken the incentives that led host countries to expropriate foreign enterprises in the past.

Finally, insurance against the risk of expropriation can be bought today not only from national investment-guarantee agencies, such as the U.S. Overseas Private Investment Corporation (OPIC) but also from a new international agency set up by the World Bank, the Multilateral Investment Guarantee Agency (MIGA). The significance of MIGA, which began operating in 1988, lies not simply in the addition of yet another agency to guarantee noncommercial risks of FDI but also in the fact that the convention establishing the new agency was signed by the major capital-exporting countries and fifty-five developing nations. It is not unreasonable to assume that signatories to a convention that guarantees against expropriation would be less likely than others to take action that would trigger the guarantee.

Given the improved climate for FDI and the diminution in the probability of nationalization, the prospects are favorable for the inclusion of certain basic principles on expropriation in any new international investment code. The principles could begin by acknowledging the sovereign right of governments to expropriate private property for a public purpose. But they should specify that in the event of expropriation of a foreign enterprise, the action should be subject not only to due process under the laws of the host country but also to the internationally accepted standard of prompt, adequate, and effective compensation.

However, formal provisions cannot fully protect a company against arbitrary and inequitable actions. A determined government can achieve de facto nationalization without outright expropriation by measures such as unreasonable price controls, profit limitations, or confiscatory taxes. Moreover, even with the best of intentions, equitable compensation is difficult to determine in the case of nationalization. The best way to resolve disputes about expropriation and compensation is to include in an international code on FDI provision for recourse to international arbitration or other dispute-settlement facilities at the request of either the foreign enterprise or the host government.

Various facilities of this sort already exist, most notably the International Court of Arbitration of the International Chamber of Commerce (ICC), which has handled thousands of cases since its establishment in 1923. In addition, the World Bank administers the International Centre for the Settlement of Investment Disputes, to which eighty-nine countries are contracting parties. Although countries were initially reluctant to submit disputes to ICSID, its case load has grown in recent years.[19]

Conflicting Requirements

An acrimonious issue that arises periodically is that of conflicting assertions of jurisdiction over foreign enterprises by the governments of home and host countries. In the past, the United States, as the principal home base for multinational firms, has been the country that has most frequently asserted jurisdiction over their foreign operations. Other countries have reacted strongly to what they regard as a challenge to their exclusive jurisdiction within their own territories.

In practice, the problem of conflicting requirements imposed on multinationals has occurred principally in the fields of antitrust, trade controls, banking and securities regulations, and taxation. The most well-publicized case in recent years was the 1982 attempt by the United States to prohibit the sale by foreign subsidiaries or licensees of U.S. firms of equipment for the construction of a gas pipeline between the Soviet Union and Europe. Because of strong objections from Western

European governments that had issued contradictory orders to the firms involved, the United States ultimately relented.

Various international attempts have been made to deal with the issue of conflicting jurisdictions. In the field of taxation, the problems have been substantially resolved as a result of a network of bilateral tax agreements based on a model double-taxation treaty drafted by the OECD. In banking, the Basel Supervisors' Committee of the Bank for International Settlements (formerly known as the Cooke Committee) has agreed on principles for the division of responsibilities among national bank supervisory authorities. Essentially, the agreement assigns responsibility for bank solvency to the country in which the parent company is located. An emerging issue is the possible conflict between the disclosure required to combat the laundering of drug money and national bank-secrecy laws.

Although progress has been slow in other specific fields, the OECD has made a general attempt to develop principles and procedures for minimizing jurisdictional conflicts and for settling them when they occur. The basic substantive principle is the following: "Every State has the right to prescribe the conditions under which multinational enterprises operate within its national jurisdiction, subject to international law and to the international agreements to which it has subscribed. The entities of a multinational enterprise located in various countries are subject to the laws of those countries."[20] In short, host-country jurisdiction normally takes precedence over that of the home country. In addition, the OECD countries have agreed on procedures for notification, consultation and cooperation designed to minimize conflicting requirements and problems arising from them.[21] We strongly endorse these efforts to deal with jurisdictional disputes and believe that the U.S. government should be guided by the OECD principles when such problems arise.

Existing Strategies for Dealing with Foreign Investment Issues

The rapidly increasing globalization of investment and production underlines the need for a comprehensive international regime of rules and an institutional framework to provide the kind of discipline, predictability, and normative assurance for foreign investment that have underpinned international trade and finance in the postwar world.

Moreover, the time is ripe for such an initiative because of two developments in the 1980s. One is the debt crisis in the Third World and the realization that the only substantial source of private external resources for development in the foreseeable future is likely to be foreign direct investment. The second is the wider dispersion in both the sources and destinations of foreign direct investment. In the early postwar period, home countries comprised only the United States and a few other countries, with little overlap between host and home countries. Unlike negotiations on trade, which were facilitated by the dual role of every nation as importer and exporter, the sharp separation between home and host countries tended to accentuate the adversarial aspects of the foreign investment relationship and to impede efforts to negotiate common rules. Because most industrial nations and many in the developing world are now both home and host countries at the same time, a wider sense of mutual interest in a stable international investment order prevails today.

Unfortunately, what exists is a patchwork of unilateral, bilateral, and multilateral approaches, some of which appear to be seriously misguided.

Unilateral Approaches

The United States is attempting unilaterally to influence the foreign investment practices of a number of developing countries as part of its implementation of U.S. aid and trade policies. Advocacy of greater openness and a more hospitable climate for foreign investment has long been an essential element of the policy dialogue conducted by the United States in conjunction with its development-assistance programs.

Recently, this country has also enlisted trade policy as an active instrument for influencing the practices of developing nations. In May 1989, India was named a "priority country" under the Super 301 provisions of the Omnibus Trade and Competitiveness Act. Among the unacceptable practices cited was the Indian requirement of government approval for all new or expanded investment and the conditioning of that approval on a number of criteria, including domestic equity participation, use of locally produced goods, and meeting specified export targets. In this Super 301 action, the United States is using the leverage of a threat of trade retaliation to induce a liberalization of India's foreign investment policies.

It is one thing to use U.S. foreign aid as a lever to bring about a change in a country's policies on FDI but quite another to threaten trade restrictions for that purpose. No country has any inherent right to U.S. development assistance; and when such help is offered, it is reasonable to ask the recipient to adopt policies that, in the donor's view, will promote development. However, the United States should exercise great caution when considering trade measures against another country because of foreign investment practices that the country regards as in its national interest and that may not be in violation of any international commitment. In the Indian case, local-content requirements and export targets are undoubtedly inconsistent with GATT, but that is not true of screening practices or local-equity requirements. Any U.S. trade measures to counter the latter should themselves be consistent with this country's GATT obligations.

In the Uruguay Round, the United States is currently seeking a broad GATT proscription of trade-related performance requirements for FDI. To the extent that this objective is achieved, a firmer basis will have been established for resorting to trade measures to counteract investment performance requirements.

Bilateral Approaches

Some 300 bilateral investment treaties have been negotiated for the promotion and protection of foreign direct investment. Almost all the treaties are between individual developed and developing countries. The Federal Republic of Germany has been particularly active in pursuing this program. Although a few agreements have been concluded between developing countries, no bilateral investment treaty has been concluded between two industrialized countries.[22] However, the United States is party to earlier bilateral treaties of friendship, commerce, and navigation with Japan and a number of Western European countries that cover some of the major provisions on foreign investment that are included in the current bilateral investment treaties.

Since the U.S. bilateral investment treaty program was launched in 1981, agreements have been signed with ten countries: Egypt, Morocco, Turkey, Senegal, Zaire, Grenada, Bangladesh, Cameroon, Panama, and Haiti. Eight of the ten treaties were approved by the Senate in late 1988, and the exchange of instruments of ratification is now proceeding. The agreements with Panama and Haiti have been withdrawn by the administration for political reasons.

Under the U.S. prototype agreement, both parties agree on five basic principles: (1) to extend national and most-favored-nation treatment to new and established investment; (2) to provide for free transfer of profits, dividends, capital, and compensation; (3) to avoid restrictive trade and investment performance requirements; (4) to provide prompt, adequate and effective compensation in cases of expropriation; and (5) to follow certain procedures for the settlement of investment disputes, including, when requested by an investor, recourse to binding third-party arbitration.

Thus far, all signatories to bilateral investment treaties with the United States have been small countries at relatively early stages of economic development. Although interest in the program among developing countries is active, it has not caught on in the more advanced developing countries. Yet many of the latter are countries in which the United States has or potentially has significant investment interests.

The problem in attempting to negotiate with the newly industrializing countries is that one or more aspects of the U.S. prototype treaty are unacceptable to them. Many of these countries do not extend national treatment on entry or even to established investment; a number are unwilling or unable to guarantee free transfers; many insist on imposing performance requirements; and most Latin American countries, because of their concept of sovereignty, are unwilling to accept the provision for third-party arbitration of investment disputes.

The question for the United States, therefore, is to what extent it should be willing to be flexible in any of these respects in order to gain at least some of the benefits of the treaty with a larger and more diverse group of developing countries. On this question, we agree with the conclusions of the U.S. Council for International Business that by showing greater flexibility, the U.S. government could increase the number of treaties and the pace at which they can be negotiated with developing countries that are hosts to substantial volumes of U.S. investment. This judgment was based on an extensive and detailed review in 1983 of approximately 200 investment treaties with developing countries signed by Japan and European governments.[23]

More specifically, particular emphasis in the treaties should be placed on the provisions for dispute settlement, transfer of funds, and expropriation and compensation. Less initial emphasis needs to be placed on the right of establishment (which would necessitate a long list of exceptions) and performance requirements (now on the Uruguay Round agenda). If necessary to reach agreement, the United States should also be willing to follow the European models in which the national and most-favored-nation principles apply only to future investment. These recommendations constitute a pragmatic way of accelerating the pace of negotiations with those developing countries that are the most promising locations for U.S. foreign investment.

Multilateral Approaches

Foreign investment lacks the multilateral discipline and coordination that apply to trade and finance through international rules and supervisory institutions such as GATT and the IMF. Nevertheless, governments have recognized the need for a multilateral regime and over the years have negotiated a number of limited international accords.

In 1961, the year after the OECD was established, it adopted a Code of Liberalization of Capital Movements. The code commits members to a process of progressive liberalization, over time, of specifically listed categories of capital movements, including most medium- and longer-term financial transactions and direct investment. In 1984, the obligation on direct investment was extended to include the right of establishment. However, the obligations are subject to temporary "derogations" as well as reservations (specified in an annex to the code) when a member is not prepared to liberalize a category of operations. Nevertheless, the code has played a useful, if limited, role over three decades in maintaining the momentum toward the liberalization of capital movements among OECD members.

A more ambitious OECD effort was the Draft Convention on the Protection of Foreign Property, which was intended to be open to developing countries as well as OECD members. Although the OECD passed a resolution in 1967 endorsing the principles of the convention, it was never adopted because the United States and some other member countries objected to some parts of it. However, a number of the principles became the basis for the bilateral treaty program with developing countries launched thereafter by European governments and later by the United States.

The nature of subsequent efforts to negotiate multilateral agreements can be understood only against the background of the deteriorated and highly charged atmosphere for foreign investment that prevailed in the early 1970s. The single most important cause of the deterioration was the widely publicized role of a multinational corporation in encouraging the overthrow of the democratically elected Allende regime in Chile. That event seemed to substantiate general allegations of interference by multinational corporations in the internal political affairs of host countries. About the same time, the developing countries launched a campaign in the United Nations for a New International Economic Order (NIEO), inspired in part by the spectacular success of the Organization of Petroleum Exporting Countries (OPEC) in forcing a shift of income and wealth from the industrial countries to the nations of the Third World. A central concept of the NIEO was the need to "tame" the multinationals.

Although the North-South conflict was the prime underlying element in debates about the role of multinational corporations, critics also emerged in the industrialized home countries, particularly among academics and leaders of organized labor in the United States and Europe. For the trade unions, the global mobility of multinational corporations signified reduced bargaining power for organized labor and the prospect of loss of jobs through "runaway plants."

It was in this atmosphere that both the OECD and the United Nations launched major undertakings in the mid-1970s to negotiate international agreements on foreign investment. No wonder, therefore, that in both organizations the focus of the efforts was at least as much on restraining the conduct of foreign enterprises as on ensuring their fair treatment by host governments.

The OECD efforts resulted in the 1976 Declaration on International Investment and Multinational Enterprises. The heart of the declaration is a set of voluntary guidelines for multinational enterprises jointly recommended by member governments and intended to "help to ensure that the operations of these enterprises are in harmony with national policies of the countries where they operate. . . ."[24]

Among the general principles included in the guidelines are nondiscrimination in employment, refraining from bribery, and abstention from "improper" involvement in local political activities. Subjects covered at greater length are disclosure of information, competition policy, and employment and industrial relations. Examples of the guidelines in the latter category are recognition of the right of employees to join unions and bargain collectively and acceptance of the obligation of employers to provide advance notice of plant closings.

Although the principles included in the voluntary guidelines may be perfectly reasonable standards of behavior, questions have been raised about whether they belong in an intergovernmental agreement. After all, foreign as well as domestic enterprises are subject to the policies of the countries in which they operate as reflected in local laws, regulations, and administrative practices. To the extent that national laws and regulations differ, the effort to establish common standards of conduct for multinational enterprises should in principle consist of the harmonization of national policies at the official level rather than hortatory injunctions aimed directly at private enterprises. However, given the difficulty of achieving such harmonization among sovereign states with different legal and social systems, the guidelines have exerted a certain moral force in setting common standards to which foreign enterprises can voluntarily adhere.

The OECD declaration is nonbinding not only for the conduct prescribed for multinational companies but also for the treatment to be accorded to them by governments. Included in the declaration is an endorsement of the principle of national treatment and the need for governments to give "due weight" to the interests of other member countries when granting international investment incentives and disincentives. On both subjects, however, governments obligate themselves only to report and consult, not to desist from discriminatory or distortive behavior with respect to foreign investment.

Recently, the United States has taken the initiative in the OECD to urge that the national treatment provision in the declaration be con-

verted from a hortatory principle to a binding commitment. We strongly
endorse this initiative.

Another multinational effort to negotiate a foreign investment agreement has been under way in the United Nations for more than a decade.
Participants in drafting the UN Code of Conduct on Transnational
Corporations include governments not only of the industrial countries
but also of the developing and centrally planned economies. Spear-
heading this exercise has been the UN Commission on Transnational
Corporations assisted by the UN Centre on Transnational Corporations,
established in 1975 to carry on research and provide technical assistance
to developing countries on issues related to foreign investment.

As in the case of the OECD declaration, this UN effort includes
draft provisions on the conduct and treatment of foreign enterprises.
At present, the prospects for the successful conclusion of the negotiations
are not bright because of persistent disagreement on key elements of
the code: whether to encompass state enterprises as well as private
firms; whether the code should be voluntary or legally binding; how to
deal with the nationalization/compensation issue; and whether to man-
date international arbitration for the settlement of disputes. A number
of less central issues are also in contention. On most of the issues, the
industrial countries have found themselves on the opposite side of the
fence from the developing and centrally planned economies.

A New Approach

This review of negotiations to create international codes for foreign
investment underlines the uncoordinated character of past efforts and
the limited results thus far achieved. CED believes this is a propitious
time for a major initiative to consolidate and supplement what has
already been accomplished in the form of a new and strengthened
multilateral investment agreement that would be open to all countries.[25]

The main obstacle in the past has been fear of the implications of
the overwhelming U.S. dominance of foreign investment for the national
sovereignty of smaller countries. Today, however, the United States has
become the major *host* country, while Western Europe has replaced it
as the source of more than half of FDI. At the same time, Japan has
become the approximate equal of the United States as a source of FDI
flows to the Third World.[26] This more balanced distribution of foreign
investment flows creates a stronger basis for common concerns and
shared policy interests. The political climate in the developing countries
is also more favorable toward foreign investment than it has been in
the past.

Companies throughout the world have become increasingly aware that there is no way to compete internationally except through both investment and trade. Moreover, much of world trade is internalized within multinational companies in the form of imports and exports between affiliates of the parent firm. And in much of the rapidly growing services sector, international trade is inseparable from international investment because activities such as banking and insurance usually require an established presence within the foreign country if they are to sell their services abroad.

At the same time, nationalistic opposition to foreign investment is far from dead. In the United States, we have recently witnessed strong pressures to resist Japanese and other foreign investment and to impose discriminatory requirements for their establishment and operation. In the European Community, too, efforts have been made, in conjunction with the formulation of new rules for the single European market, to subject foreign enterprises to discriminatory treatment. Political temptations to play on nationalistic emotions are strong everywhere.

For all these reasons, we recommend that preparatory steps be taken immediately to negotiate a comprehensive international investment accord in the OECD following the conclusion of the Uruguay Round in 1990. The negotiation would be open not only to members of the OECD but to any like-minded countries wishing to participate. The agreement would build on elements of previous bilateral agreements and OECD accords, including the 1967 OECD Draft Convention on the Protection of Foreign Property, the OECD Code on Liberalization of Capital Movements, and the OECD Declaration on International Investment.

Key elements of the new accord could include the right of establishment (subject to exceptions for reasons of public order and national security), national treatment, expropriation, compensation, and free transfer of funds (not problems among OECD countries but important for developing countries that may choose to sign), and dispute settlement (might include a commitment to use the facilities of the ICC's Arbitration Court or the World Bank's ICSID). All these elements appear in one form or another in the bilateral and multilateral agreements to which most of the OECD countries are already signatories.

No international commitments (other than to report and consult) yet exist on special incentives and disincentives applying to foreign investment. Incentives may include grants and concessional loans to attract foreign investment. Examples of disincentives are local-equity stipulations and requirements as to the level, nature, and location of research and development activities. These measures distort foreign investment in much the same manner that export incentives and import restrictions distort foreign trade. The negotiations on the new accord should address this issue and attempt to achieve a commitment to avoid adopting new foreign investment incentives and disincentives and to phase out those that already exist.

Trade-related investment performance requirements, such as export targeting and local-content obligations, are on the Uruguay Round agenda. This subject should be left within the purview of GATT rather than brought into the new agreement because the legal basis for preventing these distortive practices already exists in the GATT articles.

The choice of the OECD as the negotiating forum for the new international investment accord would not preclude developing countries, which share its objectives, from participating in the negotiations. The choice of that body rests on the like-mindedness of its membership and the extensive work it has already carried out on foreign investment issues. Both advantages should lead to rapid progress compared with the frustratingly slow pace of negotiations on this subject in the wider UN forum.

The agreement would be open to later accession by other non-OECD countries, including not only developing nations but eventually the centrally planned economies as their liberalization efforts mature. Over time, countries outside the OECD should find it in their interest to join the club of signatories as a way of demonstrating their desire for foreign investment and readiness to accord it fair treatment.

Notes

1. An effort was made in the early postwar years to link trade and some rudimentary international investment rules in a comprehensive multilateral agreement known as the Havana Charter for the International Trade Organization (ITO). Although the United States signed the agreement in 1948, it was rejected by Congress. The only parts of the ITO that survived were the sections on commercial policy, which were later adopted in the form of the General Agreement on Tariffs and Trade.

2. The services part of the current account includes not only what is normally regarded as services (e.g., banking, transportation) but also factor services consisting mainly of interest and dividends on foreign investment. Also included in the current account of the balance of payments are unilateral transactions, consisting of remittances, pensions, and government grants.

3. In the U.S. economy, services account for more than three-quarters of total employment. Aggregate U.S. sales of services to foreigners from U.S. sources (including foreign affiliates) amounted to $165 billion in 1987. Source: Coalition of Service Industries, Washington, D.C.

4. White House, Statement by the President and International Investment Policy Statement, Washington, D.C., September 9, 1983.

5. U.S. Department of Commerce, *Survey of Current Business,* various issues.

6. U.N. Centre on Transnational Corporations, *Transnational Corporations in World Development: Trends and Prospects,* (New York: United Nations, 1988).

7. U.S. Department of Commerce, *Survey of Current Business* (August 1989), pp. 50 and 64.

8. *Economic Report of the President* (Washington, D.C.: January 1989), Appendix Table B-106.

9. Linda M. Spencer, *American Assets: An Examination of Foreign Investment in the United States* (Washington, D.C.: Congressional Economic Leadership Institute, July 1988), p. 47. A number of examples of special state incentives to foreign firms are cited, including the well-publicized subsidy package granted to Toyota by the state of Kentucky.

10. "Proposal on Foreign Investment," *New York Times,* July 15, 1989, p. 33.

11. Louis Uchitelle, "Trade Barriers and Dollar Swings Raise Appeal of Factories Abroad," *New York Times,* March 26, 1989, p. 1.

12. Uchitelle, "Trade Barriers and Dollar Swings Raise Appeal of Factories Abroad."

13. See U.N. Centre on Transnational Corporations, *Transnational Corporations in World Development: Trends and Prospects.*

14. Certain aspects of U.S. tax and immigration policies are, however, viewed as discouraging U.S. investment abroad. See pages 9 and 46.

15. The case was the acquisition by a Japanese company of General Ceramics, Inc., a New Jersey firm involved in a nuclear weapons contract using critical technology. As a result of the committee's action, the Japanese company withdrew its offer. The two companies then decided to try to work out an acquisition arrangement that would not involve the critical technology. "Agency on Foreign Takeovers Wielding Power," *The New York Times,* April 24, 1989, p. 6. Susan W. Liebeler, "Yet Another Reason Not to Invest in the U.S.," *The Wall Street Journal,* August 30, 1989, p. 10.

16. Although residual controls are of little significance, a possibility that bears watching is Japanese government efforts to discourage investment in the U.S. out of concern for nationalistic U.S. reactions (especially to Japanese investment in U.S. real estate).

17. OECD, *Development Cooperation,* 1988 Report (Paris, 1988), Table III-1, p. 47.

18. U.N. Centre on Transnational Corporations, *Transnational Corporations in World Development,* p. 315.

19. World Bank, *Annual Report 1988* (Washington, D.C., 1988), p. 81.

20. OECD, "Guidelines for Multinational Enterprises," paragraph 7, included in *International Investment and Multinational Enterprises,* revised edition (Paris, 1984), p. 16.

21. OECD, "Section On Conflicting Requirements, Endorsed by Ministers on 17th May 1984, From the Report by the Committee on International Investment and Multinational Enterprises on the 1984 Review of the OECD 1976 Declaration," in *International Investment and Multinational Enterprise,* pp. 23–25.

22. However, the comprehensive bilateral free trade agreement between the United States and Canada does cover foreign investment, including provisions on the right of establishment, national treatment, and performance requirements.

23. Letter to William E. Brock, U.S. Trade Representative, from Lawrence C. McQuade, Chairman, Task Force on Foreign Investment Policy of U.S. Council for International Business, 28 September 1983.

24. OECD, *International Investment and Multinational Enterprises,* p. 16.

25. This section is in general accord with the analysis and recommendations in Donald L. Guertin and John M. Kline, *Building an International Investment Accord,* Occasional Paper of the Atlantic Council of the United States (Washington, D.C.: July 1989).

26. OECD, *Development Cooperation,* 1988 Report (Paris: 1988), Statistical Annex Table 46.

Memoranda of Comment,
Reservation, or Dissent

Franklin A. Lindsay, with which William D. Eberle and W. Bruce Thomas have asked to be associated, page 2

The statement rightly concludes that open markets are essential to worldwide economic welfare. It is equally important to recognize that well-functioning open markets need a framework of effective national and international market supervision and enforcement—a need that should be apparent from the recent failures of regulation of U.S. financial institutions. What is required is not a heavy-handed government intervention to override all market decision making but, rather, clear government-established limits to deter cheating and irresponsible behavior. The purpose should not be to direct markets but to keep them honest.

Among the required measures are international rules and enforcement through a broader and better-operating GATT, which should include new areas recommended in this study. It also requires a U.S. framework, as in the form of appropriate U.S. trade laws and prompt enforcement of those laws by the executive branch. Without these improvements and actions, the open markets will not function well and the United States will continue to need laws and regulations designed to interface with markets where cheating or irresponsible actions are overriding open markets.

Harold A. Poling, with which W. Bruce Thomas has asked to be associated, pages 3, 5, 6, 7, 10, 11

In our opinion, the CED statement is a rather unrealistic view in a world where the United States is one of the most open markets in the world. We support actions that will provide improved access to foreign markets for U.S. goods, a strong GATT dispute-settlement process, and improved protection for intellectual property. However, we cannot support the CED positions on bilateral trade arrangements such as VRAs and FTAs; weakening dumping laws; and restricting actions taken under Section 301 of the 1988 trade act. We also have concerns about the EC 1992 position.

Results-oriented trade negotiations are clearly needed to address stubborn bilateral trade deficits. While the U.S. trade position has improved with most countries, the U.S.-Japan deficit has remained at over $50 billion for the past four years. Tough dumping laws are very important in minimizing predatory marketing practices by foreign companies.

FTAs have been used for years by many GATT members to improve trading relationships. The automobile industry has operated successfully under an auto pact between the United States and Canada for more than twenty years. The results have been increased trade between the countries and decreased trade friction. So far, this appears to be the case with the broader U.S.-Canada Free Trade Agreement as well. Also, while we support trade liberalization as part of the EC 1992 program, immediate unlimited access by foreign producers could have a very severe impact on European companies. In such circumstances, transitional rules may be appropriate.

James R. Houghton and John D. Ong, with which Donald P. Hilty, Edmund T. Pratt, and W. Bruce Thomas have asked to be associated, page 17

Although *Breaking New Ground in U.S. Trade Policy* states a number of goals to which we fully subscribe, there are a series of issues on which we believe it is out of step with the trade policy this nation requires. Indeed, it is even out of step with the administration in several important respects. There are a number of the report's conclusions and recommendations that we have particular difficulty with and several important issues which the report raises but does not fully engage.

First, the report argues that the GATT Antidumping Code and U.S. anti-dumping law should be amended to require average variable rather than total cost comparisons when direct price-to-price comparisons are not possible. This would significantly weaken the international discipline of injurious dumping. It is also at odds with the U.S. negotiating position in the Uruguay Round and is more radical than proposals advanced by governments such as Japan, South Korea, Brazil, and Hong Kong. Since dumping is often associated with foreign industrial targeting and closed home markets, strong and effective antidumping laws help deter or offset these illiberal practices. We think the report should endorse the U.S. position in the Uruguay Round, which attempts to impose greater discipline in dumping and to bring all nations' dumping procedures under the scrutiny of transparency and due process.

Second, the report notes that foreign governments often intervene in the marketplace to "create" competitive advantage for their industries but "un-equivocally" rejects calls for the United States to adopt similar policies. We are opposed to a heavy-handed industrial policy but believe that the report should not be so categorical in its rejection of a positive role for government in the development of critical industries, especially in an environment in which foreign industrial targeting is pervasive. We note that the report condemns targeting without providing any effective prescriptions for responding to it. There are a number of policies, such as federal support for industry-led R&D consortia, which deserve serious consideration. Otherwise, absent effective international rules, the President and Trade Representative are left solely with retaliation as a policy tool. This is not an acceptable situation.

Third, the report points out that "Japan's industrial structure, business practices, legal system, and financial structure" all make it more difficult for foreign producers to penetrate the Japanese market. Having outlined one of the most contentious issues in the current trade policy debate, however, the report does little more than criticize sectoral agreements and numerate the advantages of multilateralism. In our opinion, the report should not dismiss this problem. If informal barriers in a particular market are high, the United States should negotiate agreements with its trading partners that both simulate and stimulate market outcomes.

Fourth, the report criticizes U.S. unilateralism (e.g., the use of Super 301) on the grounds that it may spark counterretaliation, that it attempts to remove foreign restrictions without any equivalent U.S. concessions, and that it sets a bad example for the rest of the world. At this time, however, the risks of inaction are greater than the risks of an overly agressive trade policy. With the exception of a few small trading states, the United States has the most open market in the world, and as such, we have very little to bargain with except continued access to our market. We agree that retaliation should be avoided, if possible. But the report should note that the prospect of a more activist U.S. trade policy gives our trading partners an incentive to negotiate agreements in areas such as intellectual property, services, and trade-related investment measures.

Finally, the report seems to downplay the importance of trade policy by stating that it "can contribute only marginally to restoring balance in America's external accounts." Although it is true (by definition) to say that current-account imbalances are a function of savings/investment imbalances, trade policy is important for a number of reasons. This macroeconomic accounting identity tells us nothing about the exchange rate at which a nation's current account is in balance. Opening foreign markets would improve our terms of trade by reducing the amount of depreciation of the dollar required to eliminate the U.S. current-account deficit. Trade policy can also have an important influence on the composition of the U.S. economy. For certain industries (e.g., companies which must amortize large investments in plant and equipment or R&D over a short product life cycle), having access to foreign markets can be the difference between success or failure.

W. Bruce Thomas, page 37

The selling-below-cost test was enacted to deal with the situation where price discrimination does not exist because the price in both the foreign home market and the export market to the United States are below the full cost of production. The statute provides that under those circumstances, home market prices which are below full cost of production must be ignored in calculating the margin of dumping. However, the proposal to modify the basis of calculating cost on a variable rather than a total basis would effectively gut this portion of the antidumping statute.

It should be recognized that prices are seldom set below *variable* cost. An exception would be predatory pricing, where a firm sells below its variable cost to drive a competitor out of business. It should be noted that this type of predatory pricing is addressed by other statutes. The antidumping statute does not deal with predatory pricing but seeks to provide fair trade and focuses on the situations where it is not possible to use a real home market price because of sales below total cost.

It is axiomatic that no firm can remain in business unless it covers all of its costs—both variable and fixed—over time. Presumably, profits generated during the top of the business cycle would be used to cover losses during the trough. But it is precisely during the trough of a business cycle when domestic industries and their workers are most vulnerable to the ravages of dumping. In essence, the proposal would eliminate the antidumping remedy when it is needed the most—during business downturns, recessions, or worse.

Developing accurate *total* costs from foreign sources is in itself a daunting task, and it would be a *practical* impossibility to develop accurate variable costs. Thus, a change to variable costs would in effect nullify the cost of the production section of the Antidumping Act. If this is what is sought, it would be more honest to ask for it straight out.

W. Bruce Thomas, page 49

This *theoretical* discussion of domestic steel prices under VRAs tends to mislead the reader as to what steel prices *actually* did during the VRA period.

The footnote referencing the ITC report is correct. However, this same report also said as follows:

> Therefore, the Commission believes that assuming constant market share is the most reasonable approach, but one that causes an upward bias in the estimates of the effects of the VRAs on prices and on exports, imports, and domestic sales. Consequently, the estimates of these effects in this report should be interpreted as 'upper bounds.' The upward bias is greater for the estimates for 1986 than for 1985 and greater still for 1987 because of the progressive depreciation of the dollar. The effects of the VRAs in 1987, in particular, might have been significantly less than those estimated. The bias is probably smaller for 1988 estimates than for 1987 because many countries did not fill their quotas in 1988, thereby mitigating the bias.

Thus, while the ITC *model* shows an average VRA-induced yearly price increase slightly under 1 percent, that very low figure may indeed be too high.

An independent study conducted by the consulting firm Putnam, Hayes and Bartlett, using actual price data supplied by the major domestic producers covering the five major steel product lines, showed that from the inception of the VRA until the end of the initial VRA in third quarter 1989, composite steel prices rose by only a total of 4 percentage points.

Obviously, both the ITC figure and the Putnam, Hayes and Bartlett figure show increases well below the rate of inflation. In fact, in constant dollars, steel was selling at a lower price at the end of the VRAs than at the beginning.

It should also be noted that during most of the second half of the VRA program, world steel prices were significantly higher (often as much as $100 per net ton) than steel prices in the U.S. market. In general, during this time, U.S. consumers of steel paid considerably less for steel mill products than their overseas competitors.

John Diebold, page 61

It should be noted that an inherent conflict exists between the desire to restrict export of advanced communication and computer technologies on the one hand and the objective of aiding Eastern Europe, if not the USSR, to modernize their economics to a level of global competitiveness consistent with self-sufficiency.

Often the same technologies can be used for military purposes, but in an increasing number of instances, the same technologies are indispensable for global commercial competitiveness. Just as with the question of whether strengthening the economies of these countries enhances their military capability, we must make the choice as to when the export of dual-use technologies serves our national interest and that of the West more by raising living standards in Eastern Europe and the USSR than it outweighs the military advantages it produces.

Robert C. Winters, page 66

The problems experienced by the commercial banking and savings and loan industries reinforce the value of maintaining legislative and regulatory safeguards between the banking, securities, and insurance industries. While removing existing safeguards may enhance banks' ability to compete internationally, domestic consumers of financial services may be harmed and federally insured funds could be put at risk once again.

Edmund T. Pratt, Jr., with which George A. Schaefer has asked to be associated, page 109

By its description of the current GATT negotiating agenda, this statement strongly implies that any Uruguay Round agreement on trade-related investment measures (TRIMs) will be limited solely to performance requirements. However, as reflected in the TRIMs proposals now tabled by both developed and developing countries, the scope of the negotiations extends well beyond the single issue of performance requirements. By understating the breadth of current negotiations and thereby prematurely characterizing their outcome, the statement could undermine the broad and substantial progress now being made in Geneva.

OBJECTIVES OF THE COMMITTEE FOR ECONOMIC DEVELOPMENT

For over forty years, the Committee for Economic Development has been a respected influence on the formation of business and public policy. CED is devoted to these two objectives:

To develop, through objective research and informed discussion, findings and recommendations for private and public policy that will contribute to preserving and strengthening our free society, achieving steady economic growth at high employment and reasonably stable prices, increasing productivity and living standards, providing greater and more equal opportunity for every citizen, and improving the quality of life for all.

To bring about increasing understanding by present and future leaders in business, government, and education, and among concerned citizens, of the importance of these objectives and the ways in which they can be achieved.

CED's work is supported by private voluntary contributions from business and industry, foundations, and individuals. It is independent, non-profit, nonpartisan, and nonpolitical.

Through this business-academic partnership, CED endeavors to develop policy statements and other research materials that commend themselves as guides to public and business policy; that can be used as texts in college economics and political science courses and in management training courses; that will be considered and discussed by newspaper and magazine editors, columnists, and commentators; and that are distributed abroad to promote better understanding of the American economic system.

CED believes that by enabling business leaders to demonstrate constructively their concern for the general welfare, it is helping business to earn and maintain the national and community respect essential to the successful functioning of the free enterprise capitalist system.

CED BOARD OF TRUSTEES

MORRIS TANENBAUM, Vice Chairman of the
Board and Chief Financial Officer
AT&T

ANTHONY P. TERRACCIANO, Chairman,
President and Chief Executive Officer
First Fidelity Bancorporation

W. BRUCE THOMAS, Vice Chairman-
Administration and Chief Financial Officer
USX Corporation

D. J. TIPPECONNIC, Senior Vice President,
Planning and Technology
Phillips Petroleum Company

ALAIR A. TOWNSEND, Publisher
Crains New York Business

THOMAS A. VANDERSLICE, Chairman and
Chief Executive Officer
M/A-Com Inc.

RICHARD A. VOELL, President and Chief
Executive Officer
The Rockefeller Group

MICHAEL H. WALSH, Chairman and Chief
Executive Officer
Union Pacific Railroad Company

ALVA O. WAY, Chairman
IBJ Schroder Bank & Trust Company

ARNOLD R. WEBER, President
Northwestern University

LAWRENCE A. WEINBACH, Managing Partner-
Chief Executive
Arthur Andersen & Co.

HARVEY A. WEINBERG, Chairman of the Board
and Chief Executive Officer
Hartmarx Corporation

KONRAD M. WEIS, President and Chief
Executive Officer
Bayer USA Inc.

WALTER L. WEISMAN
Los Angeles, California

WILLIAM L. WEISS, Chairman and Chief
Executive Officer
Ameritech

JOHN F. WELCH, JR., Chairman of the Board and
Chief Executive Officer
GE

JOSH S. WESTON, Chairman and Chief
Executive Officer
Automatic Data Processing, Inc.

CLIFTON R. WHARTON, JR., Chairman and
Chief Executive Officer
TIAA - CREF

DOLORES D. WHARTON, President
The Fund for Corporate Initiatives, Inc.

EDWARD E. WHITACRE, JR., Chairman and
Chief Executive Officer
Southwestern Bell Corporation

W. S. WHITE, JR., Chairman and Chief Executive
Officer
American Electric Power Company

HAROLD M. WILLIAMS, President
The J. Paul Getty Trust

J. KELLEY WILLIAMS, Chairman and Chief
Executive Officer
First Mississippi Corporation

JOSEPH D. WILLIAMS, Chairman and Chief
Executive Officer
Warner-Lambert Company

*W. WALTER WILLIAMS
Seattle, Washington

MARGARET S. WILSON, Chairman of the Board
Scarbroughs

ROBERT C. WINTERS, Chairman and Chief
Executive Officer
The Prudential Insurance Company of America

RICHARD D. WOOD, Chairman, President and
Chief Executive Officer
Eli Lilly and Company

WILLIAM S. WOODSIDE, Chairman of the Board
Sky Chefs, Inc.

M. CABELL WOODWARD, JR., Vice Chairman
and Chief Financial Officer
ITT Corporation

MARTIN B. ZIMMERMAN, Chief Economist
Ford Motor Company

CHARLES J. ZWICK, Chairman and Chief Executive
Officer
Southeast Banking Corporation

CED HONORARY TRUSTEES

CED PROFESSIONAL AND ADMINISTRATIVE STAFF

August 1990

SOL HURWITZ
President

WILLIAM J. BEEMAN
Vice President and Director
of Economic Studies

CLAUDIA P. FEUREY
Vice President and
Director of Information

R. SCOTT FOSLER
Vice President and
Director of Government Studies

SANDRA KESSLER HAMBURG
Director of Education Studies

CATHERINE F. LEAHY
Comptroller

TIMOTHY J. MUENCH
Director of Finance and
Administration

EVA POPPER
Vice President, Director of
Development, and Secretary of the
Board of Trustees

NATHANIEL M. SEMPLE
Vice President, Secretary,
Research and Policy
Committee, and Director of
Governmental Affairs

Senior Economic Consultant
ROBERT C. HOLLAND

*Advisor on International
Economic Policy*
ISAIAH FRANK
William L. Clayton Professor
of International Economics
The John Hopkins University

Research
MICHAEL K. BAKER
Policy Analyst

JEREMY A. LEONARD
Policy Analyst

Research and Policy Committee
LORRAINE M. BROOKER
Research Administrator

VALERIE DE LA CRUZ
Assistant Research Administrator

Conferences
MARY ANN GRAFF
Manager

Information and Publications
THOMAS L. MONAHAN, III
Associate Director

PHOEBE ARONSON
Sales Supervisor

Development
PATRICE GARRISON
Assistant Director

SHARON O'CONNELL
Manager of Foundation
Relations

ANA SOMOHANO
Campaign Coordinator

Accounting
DOROTHY M. STEFANSKI
Deputy Comptroller

*Administrative Assistants
to the President*
ARLENE MURPHY
New York

SHIRLEY SHERMAN
Washington

BETTY S. TRIMBLE
Assistant Office Manager

STATEMENTS ON NATIONAL POLICY ISSUED BY THE COMMITTEE FOR ECONOMIC DEVELOPMENT

SELECTED PUBLICATIONS:

Breaking New Ground in U.S. Trade Policy *(1990)*

Battling America's Budget Deficits *(1989)*

*Strengthening U.S.-Japan Economic Relations *(1989)*

Who Should Be Liable? A Guide to Policy for Dealing with Risk *(1989)*

Investing in America's Future: Challenges and Opportunities for Public Sector Economic Policies *(1988)*

Children in Need: Investment Strategies for the Educationally Disadvantaged *(1987)*

Finance and Third World Economic Growth *(1987)*

Toll of the Twin Deficits *(1987)*

Reforming Health Care: A Market Prescription *(1987)*

Work and Change: Labor Market Adjustment Policies in a Competitive World *(1987)*

Leadership for Dynamic State Economies *(1986)*

Investing in our Children: Business and the Public Schools *(1985)*

Fighting Federal Deficits: The Time for Hard Choices *(1985)*

Strategy for U.S. Industrial Competitiveness *(1984)*

Strengthening the Federal Budget Process: A Requirement for Effective Fiscal Control *(1983)*

Productivity Policy: Key to the Nation's Economic Future *(1983)*

Energy Prices and Public Policy *(1982)*

Public-Private Partnership: An Opportunity for Urban Communities *(1982)*

Reforming Retirement Policies *(1981)*

Transnational Corporations and Developing Countries: New Policies for a Changing World Economy *(1981)*

Fighting Inflation and Rebuilding a Sound Economy *(1980)*

Stimulating Technological Progress *(1980)*

Helping Insure Our Energy Future: A Program for Developing Synthetic Fuel Plants Now *(1979)*

Redefining Government's Role in the Market System *(1979)*

Improving Management of the Public Work Force: The Challenge to State and Local Government *(1978)*

Jobs for the Hard-to-Employ: New Directions for a Public-Private Partnership *(1978)*

An Approach to Federal Urban Policy *(1977)*

Key Elements of a National Energy Strategy *(1977)*

Nuclear Energy and National Security *(1976)*

Fighting Inflation and Promoting Growth *(1976)*

Improving Productivity in State and Local Government *(1976)*

*International Economic Consequences of High-Priced Energy *(1975)*

Broadcasting and Cable Television: Policies for Diversity and Change *(1975)*

Achieving Energy Independence *(1974)*

A New U.S. Farm Policy for Changing World Food Needs *(1974)*

Congressional Decision Making for National Security *(1974)*

*Toward a New International Economic System: A Joint Japanese-American View *(1974)*

More Effective Programs for a Cleaner Environment *(1974)*

The Management and Financing of Colleges *(1973)*

Financing the Nation's Housing Needs *(1973)*

Building a National Health-Care System *(1973)*

High Employment Without Inflation: A Positive Program for Economic Stabilization *(1972)*

Reducing Crime and Assuring Justice *(1972)*

Military Manpower and National Security *(1972)*

The United States and the European Community: Policies for a Changing World Economy *(1971)*

Social Responsibilities of Business Corporations *(1971)*

Education for the Urban Poor: From Preschool to Employment *(1971)*

Further Weapons Against Inflation *(1970)*

Making Congress More Effective *(1970)*

Training and Jobs for the Urban Poor *(1970)*

Improving the Public Welfare System *(1970)*

Reshaping Government in Metropolitan Areas *(1970)*

---

*Statements issued in association with CED counterpart organizations in foreign countries.

CED COUNTERPART ORGANIZATIONS
IN FOREIGN COUNTRIES

Close relations exist between the Committee for Economic Development and independent, nonpolitical research organizations in other countries. Such counterpart groups are composed of business executives and scholars and have objectives similar to those of CED, which they pursue by similarly objective methods. CED cooperates with these organizations on research and study projects of common interest to the various countries concerned. This program has resulted in a number of joint policy statements involving such international matters as energy, East-West trade, assistance to developing countries, and the reduction of nontariff barriers to trade.

CE	Circulo de Empresarios Serano Jover 5-2º Madrid 8, Spain
CEDA	Committee for Economic Develoment of Australia 139 Macquarie Street, Sydney 2001 New South Wales, Australia
CEPES	Europaische Vereinigung für Wirtschafliche und Soziale Entwicklung Reuterweg 14, 6000 Frankfurt/Main, West Germany
IDEP	Institut de l'Enterprise 6, rue Clément-Marot, 75008 Paris, France
経済同友会	Keizai Doyukai (Japan Federation of Business Executives) Japan Industrial Club Building 1 Marunouchi, Chiyoda-ku, Tokyo, Japan
PSI	Policy Studies Institute 100, Park Village East, London NW1 3SR, England
SNS	Studieförbundet Näringsliv Samhälle Sköldungagatan 2, 11427 Stockholm, Sweden